Build the Swing of a Lifetime

The best way to shave multiple strokes off your golf game is to develop an efficient, repeatable swing that enables you to hit the ball farther and straighter with greater consistency. To achieve this ideal swing, you need a clear picture of the finished product and a simple step-by-step process for building it, testing it, and maintaining it. Now you have it.

In *Build the Swing of a Lifetime*, Mike Bender, one of Golf Digest's 5 Best Teachers in America, shows you how to develop the same swing that boosted the careers of 2007 Masters champion Zach Johnson, multiple PGA Tour winner Jonathan Byrd, and 2006 LPGA Rookie of the Year Seon Hwa Lee.

Mike Bender didn't become the 2009 PGA National Teacher of the Year by offering quick fixes and compensations for deficient swings. He did it by creating a science-based, biomechanical approach to understanding the elements of an efficient, powerful, repeatable swing and devising a simple, checkable method for practicing and perfecting that swing.

In four simple steps illustrated by 150 photographs, Mike shows you how to aim and turn properly, get your hands on the correct downswing plane, and match up your arm swing and body rotation to square the clubface more consistently. He provides clear and simple guidance on how to make sure you're practicing each step correctly. Using broken club shafts, construction cones, and other forms of feedback, you'll discover how to check your alignment and posture, and make sure that your shaft and hands are moving on-plane in good sequence with one another.

There are a million ways to hit a golf ball, but only one is the most efficient way to produce shots that are consistently long and on target, and only one will help you keep shaving that handicap down toward scratch for as long as you keep playing. That is the swing you will develop by practicing and applying what you learn in *Build the Swing of a Lifetime*.

Build the Swing

OF A

Lifetime

Build the Swing

OF A

Lifetime

The Four-Step Approach to a More Efficient Swing

———

MIKE BENDER

WITH DAVID ALLEN

TRADE PAPER
PRESS

Trade Paper Press
An imprint of Turner Publishing Company
Nashville, Tennessee
www.turnerpublishing.com

Design and composition by Forty-five Degree Design, LLC

Library of Congress Cataloging-in-Publication Data:

Bender, Mike, date.
  Build the swing of a lifetime / Mike Bender.
     p. cm.
   Includes index.
   ISBN 978-1-11800-761-7 (hardback)
   ISBN 978-1-63026-901-2 (paperback)
  1. Swing (Golf) 2. Golf—Physiological aspects. I. Title.
   GV979.SB9B42   2012
   796.352'3—dc23

                        2011042290

Printed in the United States of America

To my wife, Mary Anne,
and children, Jason, Emily, and Hannah,
for their unconditional support and sacrifices
in order for me to achieve my goals.

CONTENTS

FOREWORD by Zach Johnson

Sometimes you feel as if you're being led down a certain path, and that's how it was initially with my long-time swing coach, Mike Bender. When I moved to Lake Mary, Florida in 2000, I knew it was time to bring in a teacher who could look at my swing on a more regular basis. I just had no idea it would be a fellow Iowan and a man of deep faith like myself. What's more, he just happened to work at the facility (Timacuan Golf Club) where I practiced daily.

At the time, I was playing on the mini-tours. I had won a few events on the Prairie Tour, but my play wasn't as consistent as I would've liked—I could post some really low scores, but I could dial up a few high numbers as well. My fundamentals were average, and I played athletic golf, meaning I got by on my talent and figured out things as I went along. If I wanted to realize my dream of playing on the PGA Tour, I needed someone to break me down and build me back up again and provide me with a solid foundation to work from, moving forward. Mike, having played a few seasons on the Tour and knowing what it takes to get there, was the logical choice.

Things started very slowly with Mike. We first addressed my backswing, which was very loose and handsy and required a lot of timing. Once we tightened that up and improved my hand plane, we moved on to impact and then the follow-through. We took on one thing at a time, instead of overhauling my entire swing all at once. Too many amateurs want to fix everything right now, but Mike explained to me the direction we were headed in and what I needed to do to get there, and we started to put the pieces of the puzzle together, one by one.

The improvement in my swing and my consistency was almost immediate. I made four of the final five cuts on the Nationwide Tour that season and, in 2001, won Player of the Year honors on the Hooters Tour. In 2003, I captured Nationwide Tour Player of the Year honors, making my final seventeen cuts and earning a then record $494,882 in prize money. It took fewer than four years for Mike to transform me into a more consistent, efficient player and a PGA Tour rookie.

Mike had this saying, "that what you feel isn't always what's real," and it didn't take me long to realize what he meant. Just because you feel as if you're taking the club inside, it doesn't mean you are. That's why you need swing aids, feedback stations, and video cameras, because if you see it with your own eyes, or you bump into something you shouldn't, then you know whether your swing is where it needs to be.

As soon as I started working with Mike, he put me on a plane board, then showed me how to build my own portable plane board, sticking two shafts together. He gave me a lot drills, some of which my caddie and I can use today on the range when my swing gets a little off, whether it's my hands moving too much off the ball on the takeaway or coming down on a poor plane. I have an apparatus called the Swingyde I can attach to my grip that allows me to move my hands to a nice, stable point at the top of the backswing, which helps my tempo and rhythm. Even now, as I'm writing this, Mike has me working on a drill where I swing the club back to the top and touch my right wrist to a shaft before I start my downswing. What this does is force me to slow down my backswing and help me make a full turn behind the ball so that I can fire my hands down at the ball in the correct sequence. If I get too quick with my backswing, my wrist won't hit the shaft.

The point is, every drill I work on uses feedback, because that's what builds muscle memory and allows you to make changes to your swing. There are freakish golfers and athletes out there who can do it by the naked eye, but they're few and far between, and I'm not one of them. I don't understand how you can tell a person to do this and feel that and then go out and do it. This book is chock full of drills that will train you to swing your hands and club on the proper path and in the correct sequence. I've probably practiced all of these drills at one time or another, and I wouldn't be the player I am today without them. There's no better coach out there at teaching the "how to" than Mike, and it's why he's one of the most sought-after swing coaches in golf today.

What's amazing to me about Mike is he'll give me a drill, explain why we're doing it, and then go out and do it. It's not like, "Hocus pocus, this is what's going to happen." He'll demonstrate how to perform the drill properly and hit crisp, perfect shots while he's doing it. I don't know of many swing coaches who can do that.

It's just one of many reasons why he's such a phenomenal coach and teacher. He's incredibly knowledgeable about the swing, but he's also very passionate about what he does. He loves helping people play the game of golf, and he's always trying to improve his ability to help others play it better. It doesn't matter if his client is a beginning golfer, a 35-handicapper, a mini-tour player who's trying to make it, or a major champion, he's going to do everything he can to make that player succeed. His foundation of teaching and his system can work for anybody. It's putting a club in someone's hands and teaching him or her how to swing it most effectively, and then showing the person how to do it.

There's a lot of information out there about the golf swing, whether it's coming from a magazine, another instruction book, or the Golf Channel. How do you filter out the good from the bad and what works for you? This book is a fantastic place to start. It provides you with a road map to swinging the club in the most efficient manner possible. It's not rocket science; it's the most natural way to swing a club, based on the laws of physics and what makes the club move on-plane, with maximum velocity. Mike knows all of the positions, the angles, the geometry, and the physics; he knows how to get the arms, the club, and the body into a good impact position. I don't know how but he does, and he's able to communicate it in such a way that's easy to understand.

I've been working with Mike now for a dozen years, and I hope to have him by my side for the rest of my playing career. I'm one of those guys who believes if it ain't broke, don't fix it. I know where my game was before I met Mike, and I know where it is today, and I feel as if there's still room to get better. I know he does, too. That's what this book is about—getting better. The lessons and drills in this book are the same ones that helped me become a major champion and a multiple winner on the PGA Tour, and they'll help you achieve your goals, too, whether it's to lower your handicap by five strokes, break 80 for the first time, or win your club championship.

Enjoy the journey.

ACKNOWLEDGMENTS

There are defining moments in life that shape our futures, such as the day my dad couldn't find our fishing poles and decided to take me to the golf course instead. Little did I know that this one decision would lead to my having a lifelong career in golf. For introducing me to the game and for so many years of support, I want to thank my dad. I know he'd be very proud of the career he started me on.

I also want to thank Mac O'Grady, whose knowledge of and research on the golf swing are unparalleled and who, unbeknownst to most of the golfing population, has had a tremendous influence on shaping the philosophies of many top instructors. This foundation has allowed me to help golfers of all abilities around the world improve and enjoy the greatest game ever invented.

In 1996, it was the vision of a very creative golf instruction editor to create the *Golf Magazine* Top 100 teacher list, and I want to thank Lorin Anderson for his efforts in helping so many instructors' careers, including mine. His long-time friendship and help in all areas of my career have allowed me to continue to grow and improve.

My long-time business partner and manager, Bill Tasseff, has been instrumental in helping me build successful academies around the world and a credible brand. His friendship and continued belief in our message and product make my work exciting on a daily basis.

I want to thank my wordsmith, Dave Allen, for his patience with me and all of our long telephone calls till all hours of the night, and our gifted photographer, Scott Miller. I was lucky to be able to do my first book with such a talented team.

It was always a goal of mine to publish a golf instruction book, and I would like to thank John Wiley & Sons and my editor, Stephen Power, for approaching me and asking whether I would be interested in this project.

Literary agent Marilyn Allen also needs to be thanked for her enthusiastic attitude and help in negotiations and helping us stay on track with our deadlines and all of the myriad details that needed to be taken care of in completing this project.

Every accomplished instructor is shaped by the people he or she works with every day, and I have been blessed to have attracted so many fine teachers to work at my academy over the years, including Mike Bennett, Ty Kreiger, Cheryl Anderson, Jered Gusso, and Matt Wilkes. They have been the heart and soul of my academy for the last twenty years.

Finally, I would like to thank the Timacuan Country Club and its members for all of their support in allowing me to expand my school from a five-foot area of the old tennis shop into a world-class golf academy. What a journey!

Putting the Pieces Together

According to a recent National Golf Foundation study, golfers with more than five years of playing experience have little chance of lowering their handicap more than 3 points in their lifetime. That means if you're a 100-shooter with aspirations of breaking 90, you'd better find lightning in a bottle over eighteen holes. It's a startling statistic, one that speaks volumes about the way the game is being learned today.

Now, if I chose to accept these numbers, I wouldn't be teaching and I wouldn't be writing this book. Every golfer is capable of shaving 3 or more points off his or her handicap, but what holds people back is a lack of direction and an understanding of how to get better. Most golfers work on things that may or may not be the root cause of their problems and thus put compensations on top of compensations. Their sources for fixing their swing come from a variety of places (books, magazines, online videos and forums, TV shows, and so on) and philosophies, which creates a patchwork quilt of a swing that has little chance of holding up under pressure.

Golf magazines and videos are famous for fueling a quick-fix methodology of learning, because that's what sells. Yet in reality, tips work for only a very short period of time, if at all—and they don't last! On the course, the body tends to revert back to the familiar and what it's programmed to do, because we are creatures of habit. That's why it's so important to take on one direction toward improving. Whether it's your goal to become a 10-handicapper or a scratch, you need to have a vision of what your swing is supposed to look like and move in a path that's going to get you there.

Building a good golf swing is like putting a jigsaw puzzle together—once all of the pieces are emptied out of the box, the first thing you must do is look at a picture of the finished product, because that's how you will know where the pieces go. As you keep looking at the picture, you begin to put the pieces into place, one by one, and the puzzle starts to take shape. Most golfers try to use pieces from other puzzles (methods) that don't pertain to the same picture. Nothing seems to fit or work, and the swing, like the puzzle, becomes a jumbled mess. The golfer's performance becomes stagnant, then he gives up and goes searching for another tip or piece of equipment that may jump-start his game.

When making a swing change or building a new, more efficient swing, you must have a clear picture not only of the finished product, but also of where you are relative to the puzzle. When I started working with Zach Johnson in 2000,

From left to right: 2007 Masters Champ Zach Johnson, Mike Bender, and Jonathan Byrd.

he was just another mini-tour player with dreams of playing on the PGA Tour. I had no idea he had world-class talent and the ability to win majors. The first thing I explained to him was that to get where he wanted, he'd have to stick with me long enough to make the changes I was about to suggest. Then I explained to him exactly what we were going to do with his swing and why.

Zach had the same strong grip he has now, but his hand plane was much too steep, like a Ferris wheel. He needed to swing his hands more around his body in a circular fashion, similar to a merry-go-round. This would allow him to use the rotation of his body to keep the clubface square, so that he could hit the ball straighter. I then showed him examples of this type of swing (Ben Hogan, Moe Norman) and put him on the plane board. I also taught him how to build his own portable plane board (with two shafts), so that he could practice on his own. Within weeks, his hand plane on both the backswing and the downswing flattened out. We also worked on other pieces of the puzzle, such as hinging his wrists earlier on the backswing, which helped with his tempo and sequencing.

Once he changed the path of his hands, Zach became an excellent driver of the ball and an even stronger iron player. He was always a good putter, but as soon as he began to hit more fairways, he started to win. In 2001, my first full year with Zach, he won the final three regular-season events and captured Player of the Year honors on the Hooters Tour. Two years later, he won the Nationwide Tour money list and, in 2004, became only the second player in PGA Tour history to earn more than $2 million during his rookie season.

Zach's transformation from mini-tour player to world-class player was fairly quick and a testament to his work ethic. It was also a confirmation that if you work in one direction over time, you will improve. That's what makes this book stand out from all of the others: it not only helps you build a simpler, more efficient swing, but it gives you "unlimited potential." It's not some pie-in-the-sky, "five minutes to better golf" book, but a book for a lifetime. I'm not talking about dropping a shot or two, but breaking 90, 80 or whatever your ultimate goal is. By following the blueprint laid out in this book, you will continually improve over time.

This book is rooted in the laws of physics and science and the anatomy of the human body. It's not a compilation of my opinions on the golf swing; it's a series of scientific facts. An efficient golf swing is one that is on-plane and has the fewest moving parts; it's the easiest swing to execute because it has the fewest compensating moves. The goal of every golfer is to have the simplest swing possible, because then you don't have to worry as much about timing, tempo, and practicing for hours on end. The simpler it becomes, the easier it is to maintain, and the more time you get to spend on the golf course learning how to play the game, instead of endlessly working on mechanics. Zach's swing is now in full maintenance mode—we almost never work on it, we just make sure it stays in sync. That gives him more time to work on his short game and other areas of need.

Today's golf magazines and instruction books tell you what you should do, but they don't explain the how and the why very well. They might show several drills, but they don't offer any feedback about whether you're doing them correctly. They also don't leave you with any way to self-diagnose your swing faults and habits. If there is one thing I hope this book accomplishes, it's the "how to." How do I know my alignment is good? How do I know that my posture is right or that my shaft is on-plane at the top of my backswing? What are the checkpoints?

On the following pages, I will provide you with these checkpoints so that you can gauge your progress. I will also prescribe drills and specialized practice stations to give you real-time feedback about whether your club and body are in the right positions during the swing. Many of these drills will feature broken shafts, noodles, construction cones, and so on . . . all materials that are easy to get your hands on. These training aids allow you to practice the correct movement and then develop the proper feel without supervision from a teacher.

Make no mistake, the toughest requirement in golf is to have a repeating swing that produces consistent shots with maximum distance. It doesn't happen overnight; it's a process that requires patience and practice. Yet if you understand the scientific concepts and follow the four elements outlined in this book, you will start to see positive results quickly. I know this because this method of teaching has a proven track record. In 2009, after I worked with Jonathan Byrd for only eight months, he jumped from 99th on the PGA Tour in Ball-Striking (a combination of Total Driving and Greens in

Regulation Percentage) to No. 1 on Tour. He then capped off his 2010 season with a hole-in-one to win a four-hole playoff at the Justin Timberlake Shriners Hospital for Children Open. Zach finished the 2010 season ranked 8th on Tour in Driving Accuracy, the fourth consecutive year he finished in the top ten in that category.

People always remark about how beautiful the swings of my students are. You can have one like this, too, if you apply what you learn in this book to your swing. There are a million ways to hit a golf ball, but what this book describes is the most efficient way to hit shots consistently long and on-target. That's a great way to play the game!

1

The Most Efficient Swing: Machine or Tiger?

When it comes to using a model as the blue-print for the perfect swing, teaching professionals and everyday golfers often look at who the best players are at the moment. While I was growing up, those players were Jack Nicklaus and

Johnny Miller. They were the ones winning tournaments and appearing most often on television and in golf magazines and books. Nicklaus and Miller had tall, upright swings with aggressive leg drives. That was how I was taught to swing the golf club, because that's how they did it.

As technology started to improve in the early 1980s and golfers became more fit, swings became more compact and rotary (for example, Nick Faldo, Greg Norman). Then, in the early 1990s, teachers started to look at the swing from a more scientific, kinesthetic background. The quality of video cameras improved, as did the computer software, making it possible to compare the average golfer's swing side by side with that of a Tour player, such as Norman, Faldo, Fred Couples, or Nick Price.

The mid-1990s saw the birth of the titanium driver and massive 300-yard drives, which demanded a stronger, more athletic body and swing. Tiger Woods came on the scene at about the same time, and ever since his historic 12-shot victory at the 1997 Masters, Tiger has remained the primary swing model for teachers all around the world. Tiger has won thirteen additional majors and countless tournaments since that time, and you'll get little argument from me or anyone else that he's the greatest player of this era. Because he's the best player, people automatically assume he has the best golf swing. So when a teaching professional brings a student in front of the video monitor and shows him how his impact position stacks up against Tiger's, it enhances his credibility as a teacher—at least in the eyes of his student.

Tiger's swing, however, is far from perfect. If it was, he wouldn't have made as many swing changes as he has since 1997. Tiger has had his struggles, especially with the driver. In a six-year stretch from 2003 to 2008, he failed to rank any higher than 139th on the PGA Tour in Driving Accuracy, and his distance also came down. He's not a machine. I'm not nitpicking on Tiger, because during that same six-year period he won thirty-seven PGA Tour titles and six majors, but what makes him great are the intangibles he possesses: his desire to win and get better, his imagination around the greens, his killer instinct, and his tremendous shotmaking ability. Tiger has all of the shots. Does that make him a model for the ideal golf swing? No more so than Rory McIlroy, Phil Mickelson, or Lee Westwood.

The fact is, there isn't a single Tour player out there who is worthy of being "the" example held up as having the model swing. If they all had perfect swings, they wouldn't be hiring swing coaches and constantly tinkering with their mechanics. These players should be copied for how they play the game and not for how they swing the club. Now, I could teach you to swing exactly like Jim Furyk, but you wouldn't hit the ball as Jim does because you wouldn't be able to time the swing as well. You're not going to get the same results just because your swing looks exactly like his does. It takes a unique set of compensations in a very short period of time to make his swing work.

The recreational golfer doesn't know this, however. What you have are teaching professionals taking advantage of the student's uneducated mind regarding what a good golf swing is or should be. When I use Tour pros to compare swings, I use pieces of their swings that are good; I don't simply throw Tiger up there and say, "Here's how you need to swing." I may slap Tiger's impact position up on the screen because his shoulders are perfectly square, or I may put Zach Johnson's pre-impact position up to show the path his hands travel on the downswing, but I never use one golfer as the whole model.

If amateurs were more educated, they would ask, "Where does science say the shoulders and the hands should be at impact?" But they're not going to ask that because they have no identification with the principles of science and physics; they identify with Tiger and the other players they see on television and read about in books and magazines.

The Model According to Science

So, if Tiger Woods isn't the model for the perfect golf swing, then who is?

To answer this question, I ask my students to consider the following scenario. Say you were going to fly in an airplane for the first time, would you rather (1) fly in a plane that was built by engineers who understand the principles of lift and acceleration, or (2) fly in one that was built by people who simply went to the airport to observe how planes take off and land? Of course, you'd choose number 1, because you'd feel a lot safer in the air knowing that the plane you're flying in was built on the principles of science and flight, not on someone's observations. Yet golfers are conditioned to think exactly the opposite when it comes to learning the swing. They take their instructor's word—or the words they read in a magazine article or a book—and naturally assume it's correct because their teacher said it and because it's what Tiger does in his golf swing.

Now, what if I were to tell you about a machine that is designed to hit the ball dead solid perfect every time? That this mechanical golfer is so accurate that the United States Golf Association once had to replace its test fairway because it wore out the turf, in a straight line, in the center of the fairway? Wouldn't you want to swing as consistently as this machine? I know I would.

The machine, appropriately named "Iron Byron" after one of the game's all-time great ball-strikers, Byron Nelson, was retired in 2002. For thirty-one years, though, it stood on the grounds of the USGA's Research and Test Center in Far Hills, New Jersey, hitting thousands and thousands of golf balls with the same efficient, repeating swing. The USGA used Iron Byron to test golf club materials and balls to make sure they conformed to the Rules of Golf. Today, the USGA has two unnamed mechanical golfers that it uses—both developed by Golf Laboratories in San Diego—one for testing golf clubs (balls are hit out onto the range as before) and the other for indoor golf ball conformance testing.

The original Iron Byron—copies of which today are being used by several equipment manufacturers, including Nike—was capable of generating clubhead speeds in excess of 120 miles per hour. It wasn't built by golf professionals, but by engineers for True Temper, who wanted a machine that could swing like a man but do it repeatedly with great efficiency (that is, with less compensating moves). After looking at hundreds of golf swings, these engineers decided to name the machine after Lord Byron, because he possessed one of the most efficient swings of his generation.

Iron Byron was built by engineers who understood the principles of physics and science. They were able to create a machine to hit the ball within one-half degree of repeatability every time. As human beings, we're not robots, but what is it we're all trying to do? That's right: hit the ball like a machine. We stand on the range trying to groove a repeating swing as Iron Byron does, so that we can hit the ball consistently long and straight on the golf course. We all hit great shots from time to time, and we know we're capable of producing them, but we have trouble figuring out how to repeat them.

The reason amateur golfers should look to a model that's more in line with physics is because it's easier to repeat and requires less timing. To be consistent, you have to reduce the need for timing because there just isn't enough time and space to allow for many compensations during the swing. The more moving parts you have in the swing, the less time you have to correct them, and the more talented you have to be to make them work. My mentor, teaching instructor Mac O'Grady, always said, "A bad swing gives you minimum time to make maximum compensations, and a good swing gives you maximum time to make minimum compensations." In other words, you're trying to move your swing in a direction that gives you the most amount of time to make the smallest number of compensations, so that you can repeat your swing over and over again.

Iron Byron's mechanical swing has very few moving parts and no human variables. It doesn't have a ball-and-socket joint that allows its arm to move all around, and it doesn't have any emotions or feel any pressure. With human golfers, there are so many variables that can move the club off-plane and create the need for timing. For example, humans have spines that rest in the air, held there by their hips and heads, and the moment a person's head moves, his or her spine angle changes. Iron Byron's axis remains fixed throughout the swing. The machine does a better job of simulating the correct plane and angles you must take into the ball than any human could ever do. It's built on the principles of science and the laws of motion that make the most efficient of swings possible to achieve.

What Makes Iron Byron Tick

If you were expecting the mechanical Iron Byron to wear a big-brimmed hat, much as the real Byron Nelson did during the latter part of his life, you'd be mistaken. About the only human resemblance this machine has to Nelson is the top-of-backswing position created by the large metal arm and club. The wheel and the arm take on the shape of a guitar, with an adjustable sleeve at the end of the arm to fasten a club to the unit. The wheel is the mechanical version of the human shoulders, while the post it rotates around is the spine, or axis. The wheel and the arm rotate at right angles to this post, which is attached to the body of Iron Byron (FIGURE. 1.1).

The base of Iron Byron has four legs and is very wide to support the weight of the unit and the speed created by the mechanical arm and wheel. These legs represent the lower body of a human. They're stationary and they do not rotate, but they provide resistance into the ground, as a sprinter does when he puts his foot in the block and pushes off at the shot of the gun. When Iron Byron swings down, it has to have resistance to accelerate against; it can't have the base moving all around.

So, what makes Iron Byron the model swing? For one, there are no excess moving parts. An efficient golf swing is one with few compensating moves; that's what allows it to become repeatable and easier to execute. Also, it's got a very wide base, which provides great linkage to the ground. The legs' main role is to provide stability and resistance to the ground. They move because the hips turn. The more stable your foundation is, the stronger this resistance is and the easier it is to rotate your hips, arms and upper body, and swing the club down in the correct sequence.

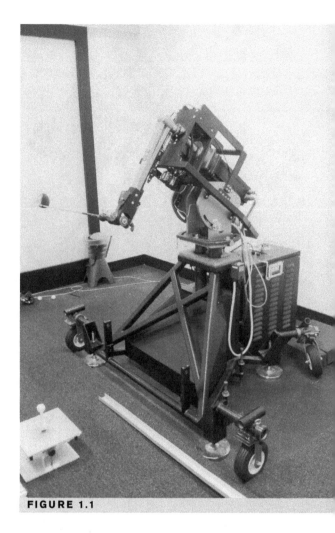

FIGURE 1.1

Another attribute that makes Iron Byron so predictable is that it has a fixed axis. In a human golf swing, the axis is your spine. If you can keep your spine angle constant, then your shoulders, hands, and club shaft can rotate around it in a circle, on the same plane. If your spine is moving around, however, then it's harder to keep these things on-plane, which makes the swing much harder to repeat. By having a fixed axis, you're able to move your arms and club at right angles to your spine, which is the fastest, most efficient way to swing an object, according to science.

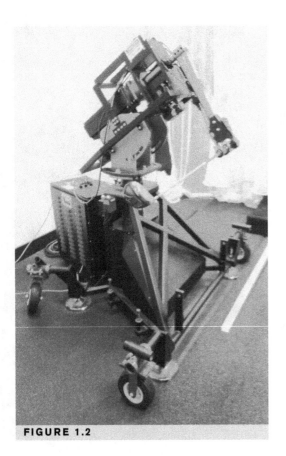

FIGURE 1.2

If you look at the imaginary hands of Iron Byron, they move right on-plane throughout the swing at 90 degrees to the machine's axis (FIGURE 1.2). Granted, Iron Byron has a big advantage in that it doesn't have elbow joints, as you do, and it has only one perfectly straight arm, but if you want to hit a ball in the most efficient manner possible, then you have to imitate the hand and shaft planes as closely to Iron Byron's as you can.

Remember, you're taking the principles that make Iron Byron so efficient and applying them to your swing. As you learn how to move your body (based on your own body type and range of motion) in a way that closely mimics the movements of Iron Bryon, you will become a much more consistent ball-striker.

Developing a Stock Shot

No one, including Iron Byron, hits the ball perfectly straight, but most everyday golfers think that's what they're supposed to do. They try to hit a shot that most Tour players almost never attempt. An on-plane swing, such as that of Iron Byron's, produces a ball flight that starts slightly to the right of one's target line and draws back to that line. This slight draw is the preferred shot of many of my players, including Zach Johnson, and most PGA Tour golfers.

It was also the preferred shot shape of Ben Hogan. He once said that "to be an accomplished fader of the ball, one must first know how to draw the ball." If I had to speculate why he said that, it's because there's only one shot in golf you can't hit with a bad swing (provided you have proper aim), and that's a ball that starts to the right and draws back to your target. If you can hit a draw, you can produce every type of shot in golf simply by changing your setup; you never have to make a different type of swing.

It takes proper mechanics from a parallel left stance to hit a draw (more about this in chapters 2 and 3); that's why it's important to learn how to draw the ball first. You can hit a fade or a slice (a ball that starts left of the target line and curves sharply to the right) a number of different ways, but to hit a draw you need to be swinging your hands, arms, and club in a circle around your body, on the proper plane. It's the most natural way to swing a club, which is why it goes hand-in-hand with the model swing of Iron Bryon. The stock shot you're trying to produce with a swing based on the fundamentals and applications of Iron Byron is the draw.

A draw is created by the natural shape of your swing and an inside path into the ball. With an on-plane swing, you have to use only minimal hand action to hit a draw; the natural shape of your swing does most of the work. The less you have to rotate your hands at impact, the more accurate your shots will be.

The Four Elements to a Better Swing

If you apply the principles that make Iron Byron work, you'll continue to improve all of the time and have unlimited potential. Yet this process takes some time and doesn't happen overnight. That's not the way learning works.

To make a swing change, you have to first learn the concepts—what you're trying to do—then be able to perform the desired moves in a practice swing. Next, you have to be able to perform the move while hitting a ball on the range; only then can you do it on the course with a high degree of success. Finally, you have to perform the moves under tournament pressure. Most people want to learn the concepts and then take it to the course; they want to skip steps two and three. It's unrealistic to expect success on the next level without going up each step in order.

Beginning with the next chapter, I will talk in detail about these concepts, which I refer to as "elements," then will provide you with ways to practice and integrate them into your swing so that you're able to achieve a repeatable, accurate, powerful swing with little maintenance and effort.

There are four elements I want you to focus on:

1. Alignment (see chapter 2)
2. Proper rotation of the body around a fixed axis
3. The path that the hands and the club shaft must follow throughout the swing (what's on-plane)
4. Correct sequencing (timing) of your arms, club, and body

There's an order to the way you must build your new swing. It's like building a house—you've got to start with the foundation and then work up from there. Unfortunately, most golfers like to jump ahead to the third story without ever laying the foundation. Take all four elements through each step of learning that was outlined above, and you will start to perform more like a machine.

2

Alignment and Proper Aim

If I were to ask you to rank the following four set-up fundamentals—grip, posture, alignment, and ball position—in their order of importance, you'd probably put the grip first, followed by posture and either alignment or ball position. Alignment wouldn't get much consideration. Why? Because it isn't taught enough, both on the lesson tee and in books and magazines, and its importance is not emphasized. I expect that after reading this chapter, you'll see just how key this fundamental is to the future progress of your golf swing.

Walk around the driving range at any PGA Tour event, and you'll see all types of clubs, shafts, and sticks on the ground, not to mention caddies standing directly behind their players, periodically checking their aim. Tour players understand the value of good aim, and they know that when things go wrong with their swing, their aim is often the culprit. That's why the very first thing they revisit on the range after a bad round is their alignment.

For anyone but a beginning golfer, alignment is far and away the most important of the pre-swing basics. No other fundamental has a greater influence on your swing, which is why I have it as the first element. On Tour, you see many different grips, postures, and ball positions, but everybody aims well. Golf is a target game—more so than any other sport— and if you're aiming improperly, you'll have to make some compensations to hit the ball to your target. Aim poorly for a long period of time, and these compensations become bad habits that are harder and harder to correct

It's difficult to play good golf with bad aim because your aim establishes what your swing plane needs to do to hit the ball on-line. If you're aiming 30 yards right of your target (FIGURE 2.1) and you make an on-plane swing, you're going to hit the ball 30 yards to the right. Of course, that's an unacceptable result; therefore, you'll start to make compensations (for example, an out-to-in swing path) to make the ball go to your target. It's normal to think your swing is to blame for hitting a shot so far off-line, yet in many instances, it's your aim. Most golfers don't realize this, however, and wind up having to make bad swings to get good results, which is a hard way to play golf with any type of consistency.

If your aim is good, then you can adequately assess where the shot went; hence, it's the only way to ensure that you make a repeating on-plane swing. Why is it so important to

Scan this code to view a video demonstrating alignment at the author's website: mikebender.com.

be on-plane? Because an on-plane swing has the fewest number of compensations and thus is the easiest to repeat. Swing on-plane, and the ball will go where you're aiming. (I will go into much greater detail about the swing plane in chapters 6 and 7.)

FIGURE 2.1

Why It's So Hard to Aim in Golf

Aligning to a target that is sometimes as far as 200-plus yards away is not an easy thing to do, especially if it's never rehearsed. This is often the first thing I address in a lesson, because most golfers (90 percent or more) aim incorrectly. There are a number of reasons why, but the most obvious is the aforementioned lack of practice and attention to detail. Where, outside of the driving range at a PGA Tour or a professional event, do you ever see anyone practicing his or her alignment? And laying a club down on the ground doesn't count as practicing aim! All it does is ensure that your aim is the same for every shot you hit to that one target. On the course, you don't have that luxury because the target changes from one shot to the next. It's never the same. (I'll explain more about how to practice your aim in the next chapter, and I'll give you an exercise to do on the practice range before every round that will help you calibrate your eyes to what the proper aim should look like.)

Another reason why aiming is so difficult is because golf is the only sport, besides baseball, that requires you to stand to the side of the ball. The difference is that in baseball, you have a very large field—or driving range—to fit the ball into. In golf, you need to fit the ball into a narrow fairway, hitting to a target about the size of a billboard in deep, deep center field. In other sports, such as soccer, basketball, and tennis, your eyes are looking straight ahead at the target. When you fire a gun or an arrow from a bow, your eyes are directly behind the thing you're trying to shoot. In golf, however, you don't have that luxury—your eyes are several feet away from the object you're trying to project forward.

To understand just how difficult it is to aim in golf, imagine trying to shoot a target 150 yards away with a rifle, only you have to stand to the side of the gun—looking at the barrel

FIGURE 2.2

from an angle, instead of directly behind it—and then fire
(FIGURE 2.2). Or try driving your car down the highway with
your head cocked to one side. In both instances, it would be
extremely hard to stay on target—not to mention that you'd
feel a little sick driving that way. My point is, no other sport
puts a greater emphasis on aiming than golf does, because it's

so target-oriented and the method of aiming is so unorthodox. Yet most people have no conception of how to do it properly.

The Concept of "Parallel Left"

To a right-handed golfer, the target will always appear farther to the right than it actually is, especially at a distance. That's because the golfer is standing to the opposite side of the ball—not directly behind it—and is looking right of where his or her body is aimed (FIGURES 2.3 AND 2.4). When golfers turn to look at the target, their eyes naturally look straight to the target, and that's where they aim their bodies. What most golfers don't understand is that the target should appear as if it's to

FIGURE 2.3

FIGURE 2.4

the right, and that when they turn their heads to look at the flagstick, their eyes are over their feet, not behind the ball. That's why so many golfers aim to the right of their targets. They don't recognize the impact that standing to the side of the ball has on their aim.

Most golfers also don't understand the concept of "parallel left" or what "square" is. When you aim, you need to take into account that your eyes aren't directly over the ball but a few feet left of it, assuming you're right-handed. That's where the term *parallel left* comes from. At address, picture an imaginary line running from the ball to your target (in other words, "the ball-target line"), and set your feet, knees, hips, forearms, and shoulders parallel to this line (FIGURE 2.5). Visualize a second imaginary line extending from your toes down the

FIGURE 2.5

fairway. Where does it point? It should point to a spot approximately 30 yards left of your initial ball-target line. This is good alignment. The definition of parallel lines is two lines that stay the same distance apart and *never* intersect. Your toe line should never cross your ball-target line; if it does, then you're aiming too far to the right.

The reason your feet appear to point so far left of the target (sometimes I hear students say it looks "100 yards left") is due to a visual phenomenon known as "parallax." When our eyes follow two parallel lines, the lines appear to spread apart the farther they move away from us. Don't let this trick you into thinking you're aiming too far left. As you'll hear me say throughout this book, it's better to err too much on one side of things, and in the case of alignment, it's always best to aim too far left.

Perception of Aim vs. Reality

Naturally, our perception of aim comes from our eyes, but what they see is largely influenced by how the shoulders are aligned at address (FIGURE 2.6). Because the base of your neck is connected to your shoulders, your head—and, therefore, your eyes—are going to follow your shoulders. If your feet are aiming to the right of the target, and your shoulders are 10 to 15 degrees open, relative to your feet, your perception will be that you're square to the target, but in reality you're aiming well to the right.

Ninety percent of golfers aim wrong, usually with their shoulders open and their feet pointing to the right (FIGURE 2.7). They open their shoulders because they're compensating for their feet aiming to the right. Now, when they look out at the target, the perception of where they're aiming is normal, but their feet tell a different story.

FIGURE 2.6 **FIGURE 2.7**

The reality is that your feet dictate where your body is aiming. They are the true aim because they are attached to your legs, which are located directly below the base of your spine. The giant base of our mechanical golfer in chapter 1, Iron Byron, is what aims that machine. Your feet and legs aim you. Most right-handed golfers aim their feet to the right because that's where they see the target—because they're standing to the side of the ball. They don't understand the concept of parallel left and thus point their feet at the target, not knowing they're actually aiming farther right than they intended. The golfer may compensate some with his shoulders as he orients himself to the target, but the rest of his body, including his feet, largely remains in place.

From this setup position—feet right, shoulders left—it's virtually impossible to hit the ball at the target with any power or consistency because you have to swing across your body, from outside to inside (relative to the target line). If you don't, and you swing on-plane, the ball will sail well to the right of your target, parallel to where your feet were aimed. Any time you have to swing your arms across your chest, pulling your hands into your body, you're not going to generate much club-head speed. It's the same with other sports. In tennis, when you swing from high to low across your body, you put a lot of cut-spin on the ball, and it just floats over the net. The most powerful shot in tennis or golf is produced by a low-to-high swing that works around the body, on the proper plane.

Feet First, Clubface Second

Now that you know your feet are the true aim, it's time to put the concept of parallel left to work. As you stand behind your ball on the tee or in the fairway, pick a target, such as a tall group of trees, the edge of a bunker, or a chimney, that's 30 yards left of your intended target, walk in, and aim your feet at this secondary target. Imagine a straight line extending from your toes to this spot. Is it parallel to your ball-target line? If it intersects your target line, then adjust your feet until this imaginary line is parallel to your target line. If it's just right, then set the club down and look at your target again to make sure your feet and body are aimed properly—parallel left. If it all checks out, then you have a chance to make the correct swing.

The feet always come first. Traditional instruction recommends that you aim the clubface first at an intermediate target—a spot that's a few feet in front of the ball—before assuming your stance, but you can aim the clubface perfectly and still have terrible aim. If your feet are aimed 15 yards to the right of where the clubface is pointing, you're not going to hit your target without making some type of compensation in your swing.

If, after you've set your feet, your toes appear to be pointing 60 yards left of the target, that's okay. It's better to err open with your feet and closed with your shoulders, because this will force you to swing the club more from the inside in order to hit a shot that starts right of the target, then draws in. One of the most important factors in creating clubhead speed and consistency is swinging into the ball from the inside. The farther the target is to the right, the more you have to come into the ball from inside the target line. If you make the mistake of aiming your feet too far to the right, then you have to swing across your body from outside to inside, which narrows your radius and significantly reduces your power.

Be Wary of Ball Position

Where you play the ball in your stance can also influence your aim. If, for example, you place the ball up in your stance, then your shoulders have to open for you to get the clubhead squarely behind the ball. Many slicers do this to avoid hitting the ball to the right. As a result, your perception of where you're aiming gets skewed farther left, which can cause you to shift your feet even more to the right—a bad combination. If you put the ball back in your stance, then your shoulders naturally close, leading you to believe you've aimed farther right than necessary.

The ball should be placed directly below your left ear for all iron shots (FIGURE 2.8) and a few inches forward of the left ear for the driver. If, when you turn your head to look at the target, you see your left shoulder, then you've aimed your shoulders too far to the right and your ball position may be too far back. If, when you take your address position in front

FIGURE 2.8

of a mirror and you look back, only to see your right forearm and right leg, then you know your shoulders are pointing too far left and your ball position may be too far forward.

There are a number of different checkpoints you can do in front of a mirror at home or on the range, which I'll go into more detail about in the next chapter. Good aim, just like any other position or fundamental in the swing, can be seen and learned. The more you practice it, the better chance you have of developing and owning a consistent swing.

3

How to Practice Good Aim

As important as alignment is, very few golfers practice it correctly. I conduct golf schools all over the country, and one of the first questions I ask people is, "Do you practice aiming?" Most of them say yes, but when I ask them how, they reply, "I lay clubs on the ground." Or they might say, "I pick a spot just in front of the ball, aim my clubface to it, and then align my feet to that." These two techniques are the most commonly taught.

Placing shafts on the ground is not practicing aim—all it does is ensure that your aim stays the same for every swing you make on the driving range. The only true way to practice good alignment is to aim at several different targets on the range, not at only one. That's how golf is played on the course: the target changes from shot to shot. You hit your drive to one target, then play your second and third shots to completely different targets—often in different directions—and repeat the process for eighteen holes. To aim consistently well on the course, you have to learn to calibrate your eyes to what "square," or "parallel left," is, and the best way to do that is by practicing to different targets on the range using the drill prescribed in the following sections.

Learning how to aim properly is one of the easiest requirements in golf. There's no speed or element of timing involved; you simply orient your body to the target, based on what your perception of square is. (More on this shortly.) All that it requires is five minutes of training before every round or practice session. That's a small investment in time, considering how important aim is to making a proper swing. Your alignment dictates the shape of the swing that's needed to hit a ball to your target. Align poorly, and you'll develop some swing compensations that, over time, will develop into bad habits; align correctly, and you'll be in a position to make a more efficient, on-plane swing that requires less timing and produces more powerful, accurate shots.

Parallel Arms and Parallel Left

As I discussed in the previous chapter, golf is one of the few sports in which you stand to the side of the object you're trying to propel forward. That makes it one of the most difficult sports in which to aim correctly. I'd argue that it's the hardest, because your targets are so small and far away. At address, the eyes instinctively look to the target, and the body lines up to where the eyes are looking. If you then draw an imaginary line through the golf ball parallel to the body, it will point well right of the target. Then, if you make an on-plane swing, the ball will not finish at the target, but well right of it.

It's important to understand that for proper alignment, the imaginary line that goes through the golf ball should point at the target. This is what's commonly referred to as the "target line." It is imperative that the body aligns parallel to this target line, which, at a distance, would be appear to be 30 yards or more left of the target—commonly referred to as "parallel left."

In just about everything else we do, our eyes are looking straight ahead at the target on a horizontal plane, and our bodies are facing the target. Our eyes are directly behind the thing we're tying to shoot or throw. Yet in golf, we have to adjust for the fact that our eyes are on a completely different line than the ball, as are our bodies. To align properly, we must set our feet, knees, hips, forearms, shoulders, and eyes "parallel left" of the line running from the ball to our target (the target line). That is the best way to make an on-plane swing that repeats, with good results.

To gain a sense of what parallel left looks like, stand on the practice range with your feet shoulder-width apart, facing a target. Extend both arms out in front of you, and point your right index finger at the target, as if you were sighting a rifle (FIGURE 3.1). With your left arm parallel, sight down the left arm and see how many yards to the left of the target it looks. It should appear as if it's anywhere from 30 to 100 yards left of where your right finger is pointing. This perception of where the left arm is pointing is due to a phenomenon called "parallax," which I discussed in the previous chapter. Our perception of two parallel lines is not of two straight lines; rather, the lines spread farther apart, like a "V," as they travel a good distance away from us (FIGURE 3.2).

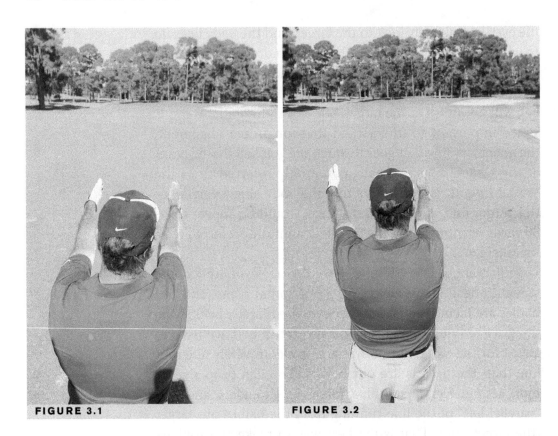

FIGURE 3.1   **FIGURE 3.2**

It's quite an eye-opening experience when you do this exercise for the first time. To understand the relevance of this exercise, you need to realize that your right arm is where the ball rests and your left arm is where your eyes and feet rest. This will help you calibrate your eyes and understand what parallel left really is.

Drill: Leave Your Aim to Your Heels

On the course, your aim is always moving around. One tee box may point you down the right side of the fairway, while the next may force you in a completely different direction to avoid hitting into a giant water hazard. Rarely are you in a position to aim your tee shot straight down the middle of the fairway. That's why, if you're going to lay clubs on the ground, the only way to really practice aim is to adjust the clubs after every shot to aim at various targets around the range. This is how you calibrate your eyes and improve your perception of what parallel left is, so that you can line up correctly for every shot—no matter what your target is.

The next time you go to hit balls on the range, try the following exercise: Pick out a target and walk in as if you were going to assume your normal aim and setup (FIGURE 3.3).

FIGURE 3.3   **FIGURE 3.4**

Then, without moving your feet, bend down and lay your club on the ground flat against your heels (FIGURE 3.4). Why your heels? Because, as I discussed in the previous chapter, your true aim comes from your feet, and, second, your toes don't provide an accurate assessment of where your feet are aimed. Any time you flare your feet out, the toes move but the heels don't. The toes move away from the target line, appearing to make the alignment more to the left than it actually is (whereas the heels stay the same distance from the target line).

After you've placed the shaft down on your heels, walk back behind the ball and draw an imaginary line through the ball parallel to the shaft that's on the ground (FIGURE 3.5). This will reveal where you are truly aimed. If the imaginary line points

FIGURE 3.5

well to the right of the target, then you're aiming too far to the right (this happens with 90 percent of all golfers). If you are aimed too far to the right, choose a new target and repeat, making sure to aim your feet more to the left of the target. Keep repeating the drill until the imaginary line parallel to the shaft (on the heels) lines up at the target every time.

Because most driving range tee boxes point straight away, it is more beneficial to practice to a wide range of targets. *Do not* aim at the same target every time or at a flag that's on a similar line; aim at targets on the extreme edges of the range or go across the range. Golfers typically have trouble aiming

Drill Bits

This is the first of four "How To" chapters in the book, each chock full of drills you can do on your own. The practice stations and the drills in each chapter will give you real-time feedback—both negative and positive—so that you know whether you're performing the exercises correctly. Perform these drills on a regular basis as you progress from one element to the next, and you'll start to see a big improvement in your swing.

Here are five things to keep in mind as you run through the drills:

1. Always have a target in mind; don't work only on swing mechanics because that's not how golf is played on the course. Keep in mind that the overall goal is to produce a consistent shot shape to a target. Put some alignment clubs down, and get square (parallel left) to your target. The better your aim, the easier it is to swing on-plane with consistency.

2. Master each drill first with a practice swing before moving to a ball. If you cannot consistently perform the new move in a practice swing, you'll never be able to do it with a ball in front of you.

3. Swing slower than usual—especially in the beginning—so that you have more control over what your body is doing. The harder you swing, the easier it is to revert back to your old swing tendencies.

on angles because the driving range almost always points them straight ahead.

As with all sports, you play the game through your eyes, and your eyes have to get accustomed to where the target is (for example, skewed to the right for the right-handed golfer) and what parallel left is. If you perform this exercise three or four times on the range before every round, you'll start to do exactly that—your perception of what square is will improve. It takes just a few minutes to do, and it's the only true way to practice your aim. No other exercise does a better job of calibrating your eyes and simulating what you see on the course.

4. Stick two shafts together and put them in the ground about 15 feet in front of your ball, on the target line (FIGURE 3.6). While performing each drill, work on shaping shots from right to left around the shafts, starting the ball to the right of the make-shift pole and curving it back toward the target (without crossing the target line). If you can produce that pattern consistently enough, you can hit any shot in golf simply by changing your setup.

5. Exaggerate, or err, on the proper side of whatever your problem is. For example, it's always better to align too far left than right or to swing the club down too much from the inside, rather than the outside. Exaggeration and feedback are the two keys to practicing well and improving quickly.

FIGURE 3.6

When to Use an Alignment Station

Tour pros always hit balls with alignment clubs on the ground because they understand the importance of aim, and they want to calibrate their eyes to what square is. Yet it's not the best way to practice aim because the emphasis is on only one target. It is, however, a good idea to set up a practice station if you're going to work on your swing.

Using an alignment station will ensure that your aim is going to be the same for every shot, which is a good way to

FIGURE 3.7

develop consistency with your swing. If you know you're aiming correctly every time, then you can make an adequate assessment of each swing, based on where the ball goes relative to your target. It's like shooting free throws after basketball practice: you keep shooting the ball from the same place over and over, with the exact same alignment, and you stand a better chance of establishing a good rhythm and making your free throws.

To build a proper alignment station, choose a target and lay a club down on the ground with the head out. Bat the handle around until it's pointing straight at the target. Next, lay a second club down about two feet inside and parallel left of the first one—again with the head out and the grip closest to you (FIGURE 3.7). That's it. Address each ball with your feet, knees, hips, forearms, and shoulders parallel to both shafts.

Now that you're aiming correctly, you'll have an easier time making an on-plane swing, hitting a ball that starts to the right of your target and finishes at your target.

A Plan for Aiming on the Course

Watch any PGA Tour player align himself before a shot, and you'll notice it doesn't take him more than a second or two to orient his body to the target. Then he stares at his target, maybe waggles the club a few times, and swings. It's not quite point-and-shoot, but there's no hesitation. Tour players have trained themselves to walk in, to address the ball, and, through the perception of aim they've developed during thousands of practice hours, with an alignment station, to swing away with confidence. They don't give their aim a second thought because they have a clear picture of what square looks like.

That doesn't mean their aim is perfect all of the time. When your target is as far as 250 to 300 yards away, it's easy to stray off-line—which is why alignment is the first thing most Tour players revisit when their swing gets off track.

Of course, you don't have the luxury of spending several hours a day on the practice range, which is why I recommend that you lay a club on your heels and practice aiming to different targets on the range. That's how you develop a perception of what's parallel left on the course. If you train yourself to aim properly—to the point where it becomes second nature—then that's one less thing you have to worry about on the course. You'll also give yourself a much better chance of putting a good swing on the ball.

If, however, you find yourself struggling with your aim or are just unsure about it, there is a fail-safe process you can run through on the course that will help you get squared away. First, choose your target (FIGURE 3.8), then pick a spot about 30 yards to the left of it. This could be the edge of a bunker or a green, a house, or a tall tree. Walk into the ball at a 45-degree angle, setting down your right foot first (FIGURE 3.9). This is the most crucial step because if you walk in straight, at a 90-degree angle, the tendency is to aim to the right. By walking in on a 45-degree angle, you open your body to the target line, which allows you to err on the side of aiming too far left. You'll also see the target much better.

Once you put your right foot down, set the clubhead down, position your left foot, and rearrange both feet so that they are pointing at your secondary target, parallel left of your original target (FIGURE 3.10). Then shift

FIGURE 3.8

FIGURE 3.9   **FIGURE 3.10**

your eyes back to your original target and close up your shoulders so that you feel as if you're aiming back to it. Take one final look at an object to the right of your target, because that's the direction you want your ball to start on. Swing away. Because the start line is so far out to the right, the club should swing down from inside the target line, creating a shot that starts right and draws back to your original target.

It's very important that your last look be fixed on an object where you want the ball to start, which is right of your target. Because all golf shots curve, there's always going to be a start line and a finish line. The average golfer looks at the finish line and tends to start the ball there, which is one reason that he or she misses the target.

Mirror, Mirror on the Wall

Using a mirror is a simple and effective way to verify that your feet, knees, hips, forearms, and shoulders are all parallel to one another, which constitutes a square setup. Stand far enough away from a mirror so that you can see your whole body, and set up normally as if you were hitting away from it. Turn your head back to look into the mirror: if your alignment is square, you should see a little bit of both knees, hips, forearms, and shoulders. In a poor setup, you will see only your right knee, forearm, and shoulder, not your left side.

4

The Correct Way to Turn

Building a more efficient, repeating golf swing is a process, and as with any process, there's a sequential order to the way you should do things. It's no different than installing a transmission into a car or building a household cabinet. You can't skip steps or read the directions from back to front; if you want the doors to open and close correctly, you must first put the frame together, then attach the door hinges. Likewise, if you want to swing with the consistency of a Tour pro, then you must first learn how to aim like one (see chapters 2 and 3).

Each of the four elements in this book has a great influence on the subsequent one. In the previous two chapters, you learned the proper way to align your body to the target—that is, your feet, knees, hips, forearms, and shoulders should all be aligned "parallel left" of the target line. Not only does this make it easier for you to hit the ball on target, but it allows your body to make a proper turn, or pivot, which is our second element.

Your aim has a direct impact on how the body turns because if, like so many golfers, you aim your feet too far to the right, you'll instinctively swing the club back on a very upright plane. This makes it easier to swing down across your body, from out to in, toward the actual target. Because golf is such a target game, you're likely to develop swing flaws to compensate for your poor alignment. In the case of the more upright backswing, it may be that you lose your tilt to the right and fall into a reverse pivot, where the upper body leans toward the target. Aim correctly, however, and the target appears more to the right, thus making it easier for you to turn behind the ball with depth and swing down on the proper inside path.

Once you have your body in the correct posture and turning properly, then your hands, shoulders, and club shaft can swing around your body on-plane, our third element. Before I start talking about that, however, here's how to get your body in the right tilts at address so that it can move the way it was intended to, with minimum compensations.

The Axis of Rotation

In chapter 1, you learned that the most efficient swing in golf doesn't belong to Tiger Woods, Ernie Els, or any other human being, but to a machine—a mechanical device named Iron

Byron that is used for testing golf clubs and balls. In part, what makes this machine so efficient is that it has no human variables—joints, ligaments, muscles—that can affect its movement and ability to repeat the same motion over and over. The wheel and the arm of Iron Byron rotate at right angles around a fixed axis, which is a small post. This post is the key to allowing the arm to rotate at 90 degrees, which is the fastest, most efficient way to swing an object, according to the laws of science.

In the human body, where the swing's axis, or spine, is held in the air by the hips and the head, it's extremely difficult to keep the axis fixed in one position throughout the swing. Even the most subtle movement from your hips or head can change your spine angle, and when you factor in all of the joints of the human body and the range of motion they're capable of producing, this makes it even easier for you to shift the axis around.

Ideally, once the axis is set, you want to rotate your body around it; you don't want any forward or backward, side-to-side, or up-and-down movement of the spine. If your spine is moving around, then your shoulders, which are connected at a right angle to your spine, will not rotate on the same plane back and through. When your spine angle changes, you're forced to make some compensating moves to get the club back on the correct plane, and that can hinder your timing and ability to hit the ball consistently.

As an example, think of a tetherball as it starts to slow down and lose control. What happens? It stops rotating at right angles to the pole and begins to wobble. Yet when the ball is rotating around the pole at 90 degrees in a circle, it's moving extremely fast. The golf swing is no different: the closer you keep your arms and the club shaft moving at right angles to your axis, the more efficient and powerful your swing will be.

Two Tilts to a Better Swing

The small axis post that Iron Byron rotates around has a slight forward incline to it, which allows the machine's arm and club to swing down to the ground and compress the ball. Without this forward tilt, the arm couldn't swing at 90 degrees to the axis and still hit the ball. Yet, whereas the club is attached to the single arm of Iron Byron, the human golfer must extend his or her right hand farther down the shaft than the left hand in order to grip the club, which creates a secondary side tilt to the right. These two tilts—a forward tilt toward the ground of approximately 40 degrees (FIGURE 4.1) and a side tilt (away from the target) of about 5 to 10 degrees

FIGURE 4.1

FIGURE 4.2

(FIGURE 4.2)—form your spine angle, or axis of rotation. If you can keep these two tilts constant during your swing and rotate your body around them, then your hands, arms, shoulders, and club have a reasonable chance to swing on the correct plane, at right angles to your spine.

FIGURE 4.3

The side tilt takes on a particularly pivotal role in the golf swing because it has a great influence on the path the club takes into the ball. It helps create the depth necessary for the arms to approach the ball on the proper downswing plane—from the inside (FIGURE 4.3). The side tilt also sets up the correct sequencing on the downswing. If your shoulders are level and your spine angle straight up and down, then your right shoulder will work out toward the target line, causing the club to swing over the top. If, however, your side tilt is in place at the top of your backswing, then your right shoulder moves down in the transition, driving your hands toward the ball and your right elbow forward. Your head remains behind the ball, allowing you to create a consistent impact position.

In any sport where an object is hit or thrown, the upper body is always tilted away from the target at the top of the motion. Examples of this would be a quarterback in football at the top of his throwing motion (FIGURE 4.4), or a tennis player about to serve the ball to his or her opponent. The tilt puts the body in position to rotate and then unwind effectively, creating maximum speed and power. If the shoulders

FIGURE 4.4

are level and there's no tilt, or the body is in a reverse tilt (with the upper body leaning toward the target), then the athlete will have to make some sort of compensation to be able to get the body in position to deliver the force.

The tilt away from the ball is one that many golfers have a hard time producing, however, simply because almost everything we do is with our shoulders level and heads up, and with our eyes horizontal. Angling the body to the right creates an entirely different view of the ball and the target. Yet the side tilt is something that should happen automatically, due to the position of the hands on the club. If you're right-handed, then you grip the club with your right hand farther down on the shaft than your left; thus, your right shoulder is lower than your left. This creates a tilt of approximately 5 degrees away from the target. Learn to establish this tilt at address (see the drills and the checkpoints in the next chapter) and maintain it throughout the swing, and you will be taking a major step toward achieving the consistent swing you've always wanted.

The other tilt at address comes a little easier to most golfers. This forward tilt of approximately 40 degrees—20 degrees from the lumbar spine (just above the hips), and another 20 degrees from the thoracic spine (just below the shoulder blades)—is what allows the arms to swing down on-plane at 90 degrees to your spine and hit down on the ball (FIGURE 4.5). If you swing your arms at 90 degrees to your spine but don't have enough forward tilt, then your shoulder turn will be too flat and your swing too horizontal. That's okay if you're trying to hit a baseball, but not when the ball is sitting on the ground or a tee, as it is in golf.

Golf is one of the few sports where you have to hit something that's on the ground. In most other sports, such as baseball or tennis, the body stands nearly erect because the object being hit or thrown is in mid-air. In the golf swing, you're essentially trying to throw the clubhead into the ground—or to China, as I like to say—which necessitates the forward bend.

One of the other functions of the forward tilt is to free up space for your arms to swing toward the ball. Stand too upright, and your arms hang closer to your body; hence, it's easy to get the arms trapped behind you on the downswing. If you tilt forward, though, your arms hang out away from your body, which allows them to swing more freely on the downswing.

In summary, the two tilts put your body in a position whereby the shoulders can rotate at 90 degrees in a circle around your spine, which is the most efficient way possible to swing a club. The two tilts influence not only the plane of your shoulders, but how your body moves and what direction the arms and the club travel during the swing.

FIGURE 4.5

Make the Tightest Circle You Can

Once the two tilts are in place, the movement of the body is actually very small, especially around the axis, or center of your body. Like a line of figure skaters moving around in a circle, the center has to make the tightest turn it can, which is why the axis must remain constant. If the axis of rotation is tight and not wobbling (that is, not moving from side to side, up and down, or forward and backward), then the clubhead will swing around the body in a circle at a very high rate of speed.

It goes back to the law of physics again: an object swings fastest when it's rotating around its axis at 90 degrees. If the inside (first) skater decides to take off in straight line, she throws the whole chain of other skaters out of sequence; however, if she makes the tightest turn she can, then the line holds its form and continues to rotate around the ice in a circle. The outermost skater, because she travels the greatest distance, moves the fastest. The same is true for the clubhead in an efficient, on-plane golf swing. Take the typical backswing: the hips turn 45 degrees, the shoulders 90, the hands 160, and the clubhead more than 200; the clubhead has the biggest circle to make and the hips the smallest.

Yet although the hips turn a very small amount on the backswing, they dictate just how far the shoulders rotate. For the shoulders to turn a full 90 degrees—as they should in a good backswing—the hips have to turn a fair amount as well. At the start of the backswing, the feel should be that of rotating your chest back as if you were turning to talk to someone directly behind you. The left shoulder moves down and across your stance (FIGURE 4.6), while the right hip turns straight back. This is key: if you were to draw a line from your right hip to your right foot, as you turn, the hip should gap away from this line (FIGURE 4.7).

The more you turn your hips, the easier it is to rotate your shoulders. At the top of your backswing, the tip of your left shoulder should point toward the right side of center in your stance, between the center and your right heel.

FIGURE 4.6   **FIGURE 4.7**

A word of caution: Most amateurs are prone to take the club back with their hands and arms because the hands are the only link to the club. If I were to give you a ball and tell you to throw it at the wall closest to you, the first thing you'd do is lift your right arm. That's exactly what golfers do—they lift their hands and arms; they don't turn and wind their bodies. The other thing that makes the proper backswing turn difficult for most golfers is that there's nothing we do in life where we rotate our bodies around a fixed head. If someone from behind calls out your name, what do you do? You twist your entire body around—including your head—to see the person. The challenge is to rotate your chest back without moving your head or swaying off the ball with your hips, effectively keeping your spine angle intact.

A good backswing puts the arms in the correct position to swing down on-plane—on a straight line to the ball. It also helps simplify the forward swing because you don't have to make any adjustments. From the top, the right shoulder moves down (FIGURE 4.8) and the left shoulder goes up—the opposite of what happens at the start of the backswing. The right shoulder moves out toward the target line and then down the target line as the right side releases through the shot (FIGURE 4.9). The average golfer tends to skip step one and thrust the right shoulder out and then over the target line, primarily because he's trying to create speed with his shoulders. He takes the club away with the small, weak muscles in his hands and arms and brings it down with the larger, slower muscles (chest, shoulders). Tour pros do the opposite and accelerate the club through the ball with their hands and arms, which is why they generate so much more clubhead speed than the typical golfer does.

Your head should stay where it is—behind the ball—until your arms are waist high on the follow-through. After this point, the upper body releases forward to take pressure off the back. The hips, having stored up all of that momentum

FIGURE 4.8   **FIGURE 4.9**

initially on the downswing, should accelerate to match up with the arm swing. This is what's commonly referred to as *matching up*. Because the most important part of the swing is what happens from waist high on the downswing to waist high on follow-through (commonly referred to as the impact zone), it's imperative that the arms and the body match up through this area.

It's also essential that your side tilt remains constant throughout the shot: this will ensure that your arms and club also stay on-plane, swinging at right angles around your spine. If you maintain the original tilts you started with, your body will have the same feel as if you were skipping a rock on a lake.

A Word about Weight Transfer

As I discussed earlier, most golfers do not typically start with enough side tilt to the right at address. Further complicating matters is that when they take the club back, they try to shift their weight into their right sides. The word *shift* means side to side, so as they turn back, they do so by swaying the hips to the right, which can set up such problems as the dreaded reverse spine tilt (the upper body leans toward the target, instead of away from the target, at the top of the swing).

FIGURE 4-10

Weight transfer is a by-product of the proper body turn and address position. Most of your body weight is on the front side of your spine, so when you tilt forward and then to the right, your weight moves with you to that side. Provided that you rotate around your spine, there's no need to shift your weight on the backswing; it will be automatic by the proper turn.

The same holds true on the downswing. As your body stays in its posture and unwinds, your left hip moves slightly to the left, toward the target (FIGURE 4.10). The weight will be transferred naturally without your thinking about it. If anyone ever tells you that you need to shift your weight or that you're not shifting your weight properly, it's because you probably didn't establish your tilts at address and maintain them throughout the swing. The weight movement, good or bad, is an effect, not a cause.

5

How to Practice the Correct Body Turn

Before you began reading this book, I'm willing to bet that most of you never practiced alignment, at least not with a club on your heels. I'd also bet the ranch that you never worked on the two tilts that make up your spine angle and your address posture. Why would you? Both pre-swing fundamentals receive very little attention in most golf magazines, instruction books, and videos.

Even if you were to take a lesson, the amount of time spent on your setup would likely pale in comparison to the time devoted to your swing mechanics. We live in a culture today where people expect fast results, and no one wants to spend upward of $100 on a lesson so that he can learn how to tilt his body correctly.

Here's the thing, though: if you don't set up with the proper amount of forward and side tilt, then it's hard to turn properly. And if you don't turn properly, it's much more difficult to swing the club with any type of consistency, efficiency, or speed.

Scan this code to view a video demonstrating the body turn at the author's website: mikebender.com.

The following checkpoints and drills are easy to perform and take very little time—not to mention that they'll cost you less than a quarter of what you'd spend for a single lesson. They'll allow you to feel both tilts, as well as execute the proper turns that your body makes going back and through. Revisit these exercises on the range from time to time, and you will turn them into habits, so that you won't have to think about how to set up or turn anymore. That will make swinging the club on-plane with speed a whole lot easier.

There's an additional benefit to performing these drills. Most people are not used to turning their bodies in such a way that they have to keep their heads relatively still and their hips centered. It's hard to do, even for the most flexible of golfers, because it involves muscles that are not accustomed to being stretched. These golf-specific muscles need to be trained, and these drills will do just that. If you feel very tight while doing these exercises and drills, it's because your muscles are not used to making this particular stretch. As with any muscle, the more you use it, the more supple and comfortable it becomes, and the better your range of motion. Keep working on these drills, and know that they're not only helping your swing, but making your "golf" body more flexible as well.

Side Tilt Checkpoints

There are two tilts to the swing: a forward tilt of approximately 40 degrees, and a side tilt away from the target of 5 to 10 degrees. For a right-handed golfer, the side tilt is a by-product of placing your right hand lower on the grip than your left; this naturally puts your shoulders on an incline, with the right shoulder lower than the left. This tilt serves several purposes, foremost being that it helps you turn your body properly on the backswing, encouraging your hands and arms to be in a good position to swing from the top. The path of the clubhead will be more from the inside, which is the most efficient route it can take into the ball.

Unfortunately, most golfers either have no idea this tilt even exists, or they pay little attention to it at address. As soon as they take their grip, they adjust their stance so that their shoulders are more level. This is what feels most comfortable to them because that's how we do almost everything in life, with our shoulders and eyes horizontal and looking straight ahead. As you settle into your address position, feel as if you're tipping your upper body to the right so that your right side forms a reverse "K." Do not tip your entire body; move everything above the belt to the right as one unit.

The following checkpoints will help you feel the right amount of side tilt, to the point that it comes naturally to you at address. Maintaining this tilt throughout the swing is the next step, and I'll have several drills for you later in this chapter to help you with that.

Checkpoint #1

Assume your normal setup with your right hand lower on the shaft than your left and your body tilted forward

FIGURE 5.1   **FIGURE 5.2**

(FIGURE 5.1). Without changing your posture, bring the butt end of the grip up to the middle of your left shoulder and plumb-bob it down from there. If you have the correct amount of side tilt, the clubhead should hang just inside your left knee (FIGURE 5.2). Conversely, if you plumb-bob the shaft from the middle of your right shoulder, the clubhead should hang just outside your right knee.

Checkpoint #2

Again, take your normal setup. If you're doing this in front of a mirror, check to see that the buttons on your shirt are pointing toward your left heel. This time, remove your right hand from the club and allow it to hang straight down. Provided that you have enough side bend, your right hand should be able to touch the outside of your right knee (FIGURE 5.3). If it barely settles past your thigh, then your shoulders are too level.

FIGURE 5.3

Checkpoint #3

Hold a shaft in place against the middle of your chest so that it mirrors the position of your spine (FIGURE 5.4). Make sure the toe of the club points straight out. Now, bend forward and add your 5 degrees of side tilt, tipping your upper body to the right: the clubhead should touch the inside of your left knee (FIGURE 5.5). If it doesn't, then your shoulders are likely to be too level. Take this a step further and make a full backswing turn, rotating your shoulders 90 degrees. If your side tilt remains intact, the clubhead stays where it is (FIGURE 5.6); however, if your right hip slides laterally, that

FIGURE 5.4   **FIGURE 5.5**   **FIGURE 5.6**

changes the angle of your spine (it tilts toward the target) and the clubhead runs away from your left leg. The right hip has to turn straight back as if you're rotating inside a barrel.

Forward Tilt Checkpoints

The role of the forward tilt is to create space for your arms to swing down in front of your body and also to put you on an inclined axis so that your arms can swing at 90 degrees to your spine and hit down on the ball. If you don't have enough forward tilt, then your shoulder plane will be too flat, and you'll either come over the top or your arms will be trapped behind your body.

The forward tilt actually consists of two tilts—a bend of approximately 20 degrees from the hips (the lumbar spine region) and a bend of 20 degrees from the upper back (the thoracic spine region). To tilt correctly, stand up straight with your weight 50–50 and your joints stacked on top of one another. Then bend forward from your hips: feel as if you're rotating your pelvis under you, which will change the angle of your belt strap from horizontal to slightly diagonal (FIGURE 5.7). Next, tilt forward 20 degrees from your upper back, just below the shoulder blades.

Here are a few checkpoints to help you gain a better sense of awareness for the right amount of forward tilt.

FIGURE 5.7

Checkpoint #1

Take your normal setup posture, tilting forward 20 degrees from your hips and another 20 degrees from your upper body. Remove your right hand from the club. If your forward bend is correct and you're standing the correct distance from the ball, there should be a hand-length of space between the butt end of the grip and your thighs (FIGURE 5.8). This is true whether you're holding a mid-iron, a short iron, or a wood.

FIGURE 5.8

Checkpoint #2

Repeat as in the previous checkpoint, only this time let your right arm dangle down from your shoulder (FIGURE 5.9). Now, bring your right hand back to the club in a straight line: it should fit your grip as normal (FIGURE 5.10). If your hand passes underneath the grip, you don't have enough forward tilt; if it passes in front of the grip, you're bending over too much. You shouldn't feel as if you have to reach for the club; your arms should hang directly below your shoulders, just as if you were a quarterback taking a snap from center. The more you bend over (past 45 degrees), the farther your hands and arms move away from your body.

FIGURE 5.9   **FIGURE 5.10**

Checkpoint #3

Stand in front of a mirror, facing away from it, and assume your setup with the two tilts. You can also have a friend or a teacher observe. If your distance from the ball and your tilts are correct, the grip end of the club should point anywhere between your belt line and belly button (FIGURE 5.11). If you're standing too close, the grip points too low, and if you're standing too far away from the ball, it points up above your belly button. If it's done correctly, you should also see some of your left arm above the right arm and both knees.

FIGURE 5.11

Checkpoint #4

This exercise works well for checking both tilts at the top of your backswing. Assume your normal setup and swing to the top (FIGURE 5.12). Hold this position for a second, then take your left hand off the club. Without bending forward, reach down with your hand and try to cover the outside of your right knee (FIGURE 5.13). If your left hand only reaches your right thigh, then either your posture is too upright or you don't have enough side tilt. Assume your stance again, only this time with more forward and side bend. Keep your head still and your hips centered as you rotate your chest back.

FIGURE 5.12   **FIGURE 5.13**

A WORD ABOUT...

Your Weight

One question I'm often asked by students is, "Where should I feel my weight in my feet at address?" The answer is: on the balls of your feet. If you were to rock up on the balls of your feet and then set your heels down, that should be where your weight settles. In this "ready" position, your body has good balance and is capable of moving in any direction. When you set up, you should be able to lift both heels off the ground and set them down; you shouldn't be able to lift your toes up. Be careful not to tilt too far forward, however, as this puts more weight over your toes and throws your swing off-balance.

Body Pivot Drills

Once both tilts become second nature to you, it's time to work on the proper way to turn and maintain these original tilts from start to finish. The best way to do this is by either crossing your arms on your chest (seen best in FIGURE 5.15) or putting your hands behind your back (minus a club). Without a club in your hands, you'll find it easy to think about what your body is doing and nothing else.

The movement of your hips is crucial on the backswing, because they control how much your shoulders turn. If your hips are tight and you're having trouble turning your shoulders, you'll have to try to turn your hips as much possible. If you still can't complete a full shoulder turn (90 degrees), allow your left heel to come off the ground to facilitate a bigger hip turn.

Your body pivot, not your hands and arms, is what starts the backswing. The left shoulder turns down and across (or to the right), while the right hip turns back. As the hips continue to rotate in a circle, the left shoulder moves across your body and the right shoulder draws back. The hips continue to turn until the tip of your left shoulder points to the right of center in your stance (FIGURE 5.14), an indication that your shoulders have rotated a full 90 degrees.

FIGURE 5.14

The depth of your hands on your backswing comes from your body pivot (FIGURE 5.15) and the height from the fact you're tilted forward and your right elbow bends. Most people have only the height because they don't turn properly or don't set up in the correct tilts. If you allow your hands to move with your pivot, then your hands will have the proper depth.

The whole purpose of the backswing pivot is to create the proper depth and the optimum position of the hands and arms to swing down from the top. In the transition, the first move down is when the hands fire at the golf ball; therefore, the right shoulder will move down before moving out to the target line (FIGURE 5.16). The average golfer's right shoulder

FIGURE 5.15   **FIGURE 5.16**

first moves out toward the target line, instead of down, which causes the shoulders to come over the top. At impact, your upper body essentially resets to where it was at address, with both tilts remaining intact and your hips open to the target line (FIGURE 5.17). Through impact, the right shoulder moves down the target line and your head stays back, behind the ball—until your arms are waist high in the follow-through, when your head releases forward to take pressure off your back. Your swing is basically over with by the time your arms have reached waist high in the follow-through, the momentum pulling your body around into a full finish (FIGURE 5.18). The following four drills will greatly enhance your ability to

FIGURE 5.17

FIGURE 5.18

Wall Drills

FIGURE 5.19

FIGURE 5.20

turn correctly, while also increasing your flexibility. The goal is to keep your head relatively still and your hips turning in a circle, rather than swaying from side to side. If you can control the top and the bottom of your spine, then you have a reasonable chance at keeping both tilts intact and rotating around your axis in the most efficient manner possible—with your arms, hands, and club shaft all at right angles to your spine.

Drill #1: Touch Your Hands to the Wall

Pretend you're holding a club and get into your normal golf posture, your rear end lightly touching a wall (not pressing into it). Keeping your head steady, rotate your hips and chest straight back until you can touch the wall with your hands (FIGURE 5.19). Your left arm should be extended and your head in the same position it was at address. Don't allow your head to go with your body (sway) in order to touch the wall; turn your shoulders to get the depth (FIGURE 5.20). You should feel a good stretch in your left side and most of your weight over your right leg when your hands meet the wall.

FIGURE 5.21

FIGURE 5.22

Drill #2: Press Your Hips into the Wall

Assume your normal setup posture with your hands behind your back and the outside of your left foot up against a wall. Rotate your hips and shoulders back, as if you were making a backswing (FIGURE 5.21), then turn through into a finish position, pushing your hips into the wall. Your chest should be about a foot away from the wall at this point, an indication that your spine angle to the right is still intact (FIGURE 5.22). Many golfers lose this angle and come over the top of the ball on the downswing (from outside to inside). Maintaining this side tilt is key to swinging the club down on the proper plane, from the inside.

FIGURE 5.23   FIGURE 5.24

Drill #3: Extend and Touch the Wall

Here's another drill to train you how to keep your side tilt intact. Set up with your left hip about a foot and a half to two feet from a wall—far enough that you can extend your right arm and touch the wall. Extend your left arm out away from your body, balancing it on a club (FIGURE 5.23). Take an imaginary grip with your right hand, then turn your body back and through, swinging your right arm down and underneath the left. Extend the arm into the wall and press your hand flat against it (FIGURE 5.24). Your right arm should be straight and your wrist bent; more important, your head should be back and your spine still tilted to the right.

Drill #4: Turn inside the Wall

Hold a shaft up high across your shoulders and get into your golf posture. Make sure the grip end of the club is touching the wall or extending just past the door frame (FIGURE 5.25), and take your normal backswing. On the downswing, move your hips laterally and the right shoulder down (not out), so that the grip end of the club swings up and misses the wall (FIGURE 5.26). At the finish, your hips should almost be touching the wall, with your weight over your front leg (FIGURE 5.27). This drill not only helps you stay in both tilts, but also teaches you how to rotate around your spine and swing your hands and club on the proper downswing plane. It's great for people who have a tendency to spin out with their hips (on the downswing) and come over the top with their shoulders.

FIGURE 5.25

FIGURE 5.26

FIGURE 5.27

Swing Length

Provided that you maintain both tilts, you should have good width and length to your backswing, and you shouldn't be able to overswing. Just what is the right length for your swing? Here's a test: Hold your left arm straight out in front of you, then move it across your chest as far as you can without bending your arm. Hold it there. Assume your golf posture, then rotate your shoulders a full 90 degrees. Add your right hand to the left to form a normal grip. That's the proper radius (a measurement of the distance between your left shoulder and the butt end of the club) and the length you should have to your backswing. To swing the club any farther back, you'd have to overbend your elbows or lose your tilts, compromising your swing's radius and weakening your efficiency and power potential.

Hitting Drills

The following three hitting drills are designed to give you immediate feedback so that you know whether you're turning your body properly and maintaining your tilts. The shafts can be found at any club repair shop or location where clubs are built; likewise, you can find the noodles at any swimming supply store or place where swimming supplies are sold, such as Target or Walmart. Always put the clubs down on the ground for alignment any time you're working on your swing. When performing these drills for the first time, start by hitting some tees out of the ground before you advance to balls.

Drill #1: Don't Drop the Ball

Put two shafts together, and slide a noodle onto the grip end of the top shaft. Stick both shafts in the ground at an angle (toward you), then take your address position with the right side of your head lightly touching the noodle. Make sure you set up with both tilts. Tee up a ball, then put a second tee in the ground to mark your ball position. Next, lodge a third shaft—or you could also use the back of a chair—in the ground just outside your right hip and slide a peg into the end of the grip. Place a ball on that tee (FIGURE 5.28). Now you're ready. Make a swing, turning your right hip away from the shaft on the backswing and keeping your head against the noodle at all times (FIGURE 5.29). If you can control your hips and the top of your spine (your head), then you should maintain your tilts.

Most amateurs have a hard time maintaining the side tilt, especially on the backswing. The hips shift laterally instead of turning, knocking the ball off the tee. On the backswing, your right hip needs to turn straight back, inside the shaft, creating a gap between the shaft and your

FIGURE 5.28

FIGURE 5.29

hip. As you transition and swing forward, keep your head back against the noodle for as long as you can. If either tilt is compromised, it will be hard to maintain contact with the noodle.

Drill #2: Noodle on the Left Ear

Set up with the two shafts and the noodle positioned just off your left ear (FIGURE 5.30). Again, put a second tee in the ground to mark your ball position. The goal here is to make some swings while keeping your head just behind the noodle as you swing to waist high on the follow-through, or

FIGURE 5.30

until your arms are parallel to the ground (FIGURE 5.31). The noodle helps preserve your side tilt on the downswing, so that you don't spin out or try to hit the ball with your upper body. Provided that the tilt remains, your arms will swing down to the ball on the proper path, from the inside.

You can make this drill more challenging by placing a third shaft, or a chair, in the ground just outside your left hip. On the backswing, your left hip should stay on the shaft; it should not gap away. On the downswing, push your left hip into the shaft and continue to apply some light pressure to it until your hands, arms, and club are waist high on the follow-through.

FIGURE 5.31

Drill #3: Turn over the Chair

Place a chair beside you so that the back is just behind your right thigh. Now take your normal setup but without a club (FIGURE 5.32). Rotate back and bend over the top of the chair to pick up a pillow you left on the seat of the chair (FIGURE 5.33). You should feel as if your upper body is rotating over the top of the chair, while your eyes and head remain looking at the ball. Lift the pillow up with your arms and hold it above your right shoulder as you would a club (FIGURE 5.34).

FIGURE 5.32

FIGURE 5.33

FIGURE 5.34   **FIGURE 5.35**

Now try to feel the same thing with a golf club. Repeat the exercise, recreating the same feeling of turning your upper body over the chair on the backswing (FIGURE 5.35). Then swing on down and through. This drill encourages you to swing around your spine without swaying your hips into the chair; it also prevents you from overswinging because when you're bent over the chair, you can't swing your arms any farther back. Overswinging, in many cases, causes you to lose your spine angle.

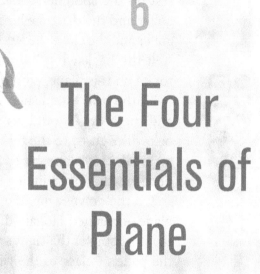

6

The Four Essentials of Plane

Most golfers' definition of "swing plane" is that of a straight line drawn right through the shaft at address, or Ben Hogan's famous image of the pane of glass angled from the top of the shoulders to the ball. Their concept of what is "on-plane" relates only to the club shaft, and whether it travels along these lines on the backswing and the downswing.

Yet Hogan wasn't referring only to the shaft of the club with his pane of glass image; rather, he was talking about the angle the shoulders must take on the backswing. In his book *Ben Hogan's Five Lessons: The Modern Fundamentals of Golf,* Hogan discussed two different planes in the golf swing—one for the backswing and another for the downswing. The angle of the glass, which had a hole cut through it so that it could rest on the shoulders, was determined by the height of the golfer and the distance he stood from the ball. The taller the golfer and the closer he stood to the ball, the steeper the angle. "On the backswing," wrote Hogan, "the shoulders should rotate on this plane, continuously inclined at the same angle [with the ball] established at address." As a result, the hands and the arms "should remain parallel with the plane [just below the glass] to the top of the backswing." They were not to break this plane by swinging too upright, or drop well underneath it by swinging too flat.

Scan this code to view a video demonstrating the swing plane at the author's website: mikebender.com.

On the downswing, the club moved on a much shallower plane, explained Hogan, due to the rotation of the hips and the dropping of the right shoulder. This would affectively tilt the pane of glass to the right and force the golfer to swing more from the inside out, never breaking the glass. The pane of glass was a barrier that could not be broken on either the backswing or the downswing.

In his book *The Plane Truth for Golfers,* Jim Hardy introduced another popular concept about plane, which underlined the differences between a one-plane swing and a two-plane swing. In a one-plane swing, the left arm travels on the same angle as the shoulders throughout the swing. The arms swing along your body in a rotary fashion, instead of up and down. In a two-plane swing, the left arm swings on a higher plane than the line of the shoulders; in other words, the body is turning in one circle and the hands and the arms in another.

As these books show, a variety of opinions are out there regarding what constitutes the swing plane, but that isn't all there is to know. In actuality, we need to consider four things when it comes to being on-plane: in addition to the plane the shaft moves on, there's the optimum path the hands travel on, the angle the shoulders rotate on, and the angle the club-face swings on. Each one has a particular path it must move in around your swing's axis, which is the spine, in order for your swing to meet the definition of being "on-plane."

In this chapter, I'll take a closer look at all four of these considerations for plane, starting with the most crucial one—the hand path. I will explain how each should move in space. The next chapter will show you how to get everything on-plane, with checkpoints and drills that will allow you to see and feel what is on-plane and what's not.

Hand Path: Take a Straight Line into the Ball

The reason I believe the path of the hands is the most impor-tant concept to understand is because they control where the shaft goes and what the clubface does. If the hands move around the body on the correct path, you'll consistently arrive at a good impact position. If your hands are not on the correct plane, you'll need more compensations to get back to a good impact position.

The correct hand path takes on the shape of a half moon—a semicircular arc on the backswing, followed by a straight line into impact. Your hands should remain on the original shaft plane—the angle of the shaft at address—until they reach waist height on the backswing, at which point the right elbow starts to bend (FIGURE 6.1). This makes the hands go up, along with the tilting of the shoulders at address. The hands move more up toward the end of the backswing than they do in the beginning (FIGURE 6.2). On the downswing, they make a beeline toward the golf ball—provided that they arrive at the

FIGURE 6.1   **FIGURE 6.2**

top of the backswing with the left arm parallel to your shoulders, ninety degrees to your spine.

Your hand position at the top determines the starting point of the downswing and thus has a great influence on how much clubhead speed you're capable of generating. If, as described earlier, the hands are on-plane at the top of the backswing, then they're in the optimum position to attack the ball. They can take a straight line into the ball with minimum compensations, which is the fastest route possible between the two points (FIGURES 6.3, 6.4, AND 6.5). If your hands are out of position at the top, then you have to reroute them to get back on-plane in a very short period of time—about a quarter of a second—and that's not too easy to repeat. From the top, you want to release the clubhead straight into the back of the ball—commonly referred to as straight-line acceleration—which is the most efficient and powerful way to bring the club down.

The other reason the hand path is so important is because the shaft follows the direction of the hands, which pulls it in a straight line. You can have your hands and arms anywhere in space and still have the shaft on-plane on the backswing, but for it to be tracking in a straight line to the ball on the downswing, your hands must be moving in a straight line as well. The shaft will go where your hands go because they're pulling on the end of the handle. Centrifugal forces take over from there, pulling the shaft down in the same direction.

Similar to putting, the more you keep your hands on the right path, the less you have to manipulate the clubface with

FIGURE 6.3

FIGURE 6.4

FIGURE 6.5

your hands to hit the ball on target. If your hands are under plane (swinging out to the right) or over it (swinging to the left), then you start to rely less on physics and more on strength and luck to hit the ball where you want it to go. Every now and then, you might time it just right and hit a perfect shot, but that's luck, not the result of making a good golf swing.

To illustrate just how important the hand path is, all one has to do is examine the swing of 2010 FedEx Cup champion Jim Furyk. Traditionally one of the game's most accurate drivers and iron players, Furyk has a swing that is anything but conventional. He takes the clubhead back to the outside and then lifts his arms vertically to the top, pulling his hands and shaft way off-plane. But then he quickly loops his hands and club back to the inside at the start of the downswing to get them back on-plane. This one magic move puts his hands in the proper position to hit the ball from the inside, something all great ball-strikers do.

Shaft Plane: Locate the Target Line

The angle of the shaft at address is often thought of as the proper angle in regard to the swing plane, but that's not true. For the shaft to meet the definition of being on-plane, it must be pointing at or parallel to the target line (or an extension of this line) at all times during the swing. The target line stretches from the ball to the target and also extends behind the ball to infinity, so if the shaft points to a spot 20 yards in front of or behind the ball and it's on the target line, then the shaft is considered to be on-plane. Whichever end of the club is closest to the ground, whether it's the hosel or the butt end of the grip, it should always point to this line or be parallel to it (FIGURES 6.6, 6.7, 6.8, AND 6.9).

FIGURE 6.6

FIGURE 6.7

FIGURE 6.8

FIGURE 6.9

The shaft is either on-plane, over the plane, or underneath the plane at all points in the swing. When someone says you're over the plane, however, he is usually referring to the downswing. If you're over the plane, you are exactly that—the butt end of the shaft is pointing outside the target line coming down. This is frequently the result of your sequencing being off at the start of the downswing: the right shoulder moves out, not down, throwing the hands and the club out over the target line and causing you to swing across your body from right to left (FIGURE 6.10). A number of other things can cause

FIGURE 6.10

you to be over the plane on the downswing—aiming too far to the right of the target, not getting enough depth on your backswing, or lifting your arms to the top—but poor sequencing is usually to blame (SEE CHAPTER 8).

Most amateurs swing the shaft over the plane. Those who swing it under the plane on the downswing are approaching the ball too much from the inside, from left to right. Someone who does this either drops his hands down too vertically—instead of moving them toward the ball—or moves his pelvis in toward the ball, thus losing his forward tilt and increasing the amount of side bend. The latter is called changing tilts, or tilting out, which causes the hands and the club shaft to drop under the plane. This move is usually found in better golfers and is a compensation for either a poor backswing or bad sequencing at the start of the downswing. All good players find a way to hit the ball from the inside, and that is why swinging under the plane—or too shallow—is usually a better player's mistake.

Shoulder Plane: Control Your Spine

Your shoulders are connected to your spine at right angles, and thus will always rotate around your spine at 90 degrees. That is undeniable. Yet the path your shoulders travel on isn't as simple, and is greatly influenced by your body's tilts at address and whether you're able to sustain these throughout the swing.

For your shoulders to stay on-plane on either the backswing or the downswing, your spine angle needs to remain constant. If there's any side-to-side, forward-and-backward, or up-and-down movement to your spine, then the axis changes and so does the angle your shoulders rotate on. For example, if you were to come up out of your spine angle on the downswing, your shoulder turn would become too flat, and you would very likely contact the top of the ball (hit the shot too thin); if the base of your spine slid too aggressively toward the target on the downswing, then your weight would fall back and your shoulders would take too steep of an approach into the ball. In this instance, you'd probably hit the shot fat. Maintain your forward and side tilts, and your shoulders will go where they have to go.

If you were to draw a box around your upper body at address (angled to match your forward spine tilt), your shoulders would rotate inside this box (FIGURES 6.11 AND 6.12). Think of the image of turning your hips inside a barrel, only apply it

FIGURE 6.11

FIGURE 6.12

to your shoulders—on an inclined angle—to keep the shoulders moving on-plane.

Clubface Plane: Avoid the Extremes

The clubface angle is the least important of the four considerations for plane, because it's solely responsible for what your hands have to do to return the face to square at impact. The hands control the clubface, which is why someone with an extremely strong grip (V's formed by thumbs and forefingers pointing to the right of the right shoulder), such as Zach Johnson, can still play great golf. Zach's clubface is closed at the top, yet he's able to hit a consistent 5-yard draw because his hands are on the correct path and he's grooved his release habit so well.

You should be concerned about the face only if it's extremely open or closed at the top of your backswing. These two extremes can create problems for the release at the bottom of your swing. If the clubface is on the open side—or points toward the ground—your hands have to rotate more to square the face; if the clubface is closed with the face pointing up toward the sky, your hands have to hold on more. Johnson's swing would be an example of the latter. At the top, his clubface is slightly closed, so he doesn't have to rotate the face at all to get into a good impact position. He just hangs onto the release and thus hits the ball with a slight draw all day long.

Different amounts of rotation are required to make the ball go straight: the weaker your grip (V's pointing more toward your chin), the more wrist rotation you need; the stronger your grip, the less you need. The optimal clubface position at the top of the backswing is parallel to your left forearm, and coming through (post-impact) it should match your spine angle. (Refer again to FIGURES 6.11 AND 6.12.) Those are the two checkpoints with the clubface you should be most concerned with. You want the rotation of the face to happen before the ball because the unhinging and rotation of the wrists create speed; you want to minimize the amount of wrist rotation after impact.

The Biggest Threat to Swinging On-Plane

You can have your hands and arms anywhere in space and still have the shaft on-plane. That's because your arms are attached to a ball-and-socket joint and have a full range of motion; the wrists can turn in many different directions as well. All of these things challenge your ability to keep everything moving on-plane.

The golf swing would be a heck of a lot easier if you had limited joints, as Iron Byron does (see chapter 1). The machine's arms can swing only one way, which is why it's so efficient—it has the fewest number of moving parts possible. The goal in the human swing is to train your joints to move in the fewest ways possible. If you allow your hands and arms to be moved by your pivot around your body, and you maintain your original spine angle throughout the swing, you will have a more consistent, repeating swing.

7

How to Establish an On-Plane Swing

Now that you know there's more to the term *plane* than simply what the club is doing, it's time to practice all four considerations for plane. The checkpoints that follow will allow you to see where your hands, club shaft, shoulders, and clubface need to be in space in order to be on-plane, based on the laws of physics and science as they relate to the human body. For many golfers, what they see and what they "should" see are two completely different things. These checkpoints will provide you with the framework that's necessary to build an on-plane swing with the fewest moving parts, which is the most efficient swing attainable.

The drills and the accompanying stations in this chapter will teach you how to move your body and the club in space by exaggerating on the correct side of what is on-plane. This is done through the use of shafts, noodles, road cones, and other obstacles that force your hands and the club shaft onto the right path as you're hitting balls. The whole idea when practicing is to create feedback so that you know when you're doing something right or wrong. The drills are designed to do just that and to get everything moving on the correct plane.

Checkpoints for the Hand Path

The most essential of the four considerations for plane is the path of the hands, bar none. In fact, I'd argue that it's the most important aspect of the golf swing. The comparison I make is to that of the hands in putting. The hands travel on a very small arc in the putting stroke, and provided that they stay on-plane, the putterface will likely be square at impact; you won't have to manipulate the face in any way. It's much the same with the hands on the full swing: while the arc the hands take is much bigger, as long as they stay on-plane, you're going to require fewer compensations to hit a good shot. The club follows the hands wherever they go, and if you can get your hands in the correct position at the top (to attack the ball in a straight line), you will hit the ball efficiently with speed.

Work on the following checkpoints for the hand path at home, in front of a mirror, or on the practice range. When on the range, make sure to set up your alignment station first so that you have a reference point for what your target line is.

Figure 1: As Zach Johnson demonstrates here, your hands should swing back along the original shaft plane (the angle of the shaft when the clubhead is soled at address) until the shaft is parallel to the ground. At this point, your hands should blend in with your left thigh (FIGURE 7.1). If you suck the clubhead too far to the inside, as most amateurs do, your hands will be behind your left thigh.

FIGURE 7.1

Figure 2: Zach continues to rotate back in his spine angle until his arms are parallel to the ground. For your hands to be on-plane at this point, they should be even with your right bicep (FIGURE 7.2); your arms should also be on a 45-degree angle to the target line. If your hands are behind your bicep, in the middle of your chest, or out away from your body, then they're not on-plane.

FIGURE 7.2

FIGURE 7.3

FIGURE 7.4

Figure 3: At the top of the backswing, your left arm and hands should be on the same line as your shoulders, as Zach's are (FIGURE 7.3). If your arm is above or below this line, then your hands are off-plane. It is crucial that you master this position because if your hands are on-plane at the top, they can take a straight line into the ball. This straight-line acceleration is a must if you want to maximize your clubhead speed. (Note: Players who have limited flexibility and shorter arms may be slightly lower than the shoulder line at the top.)

Figure 4: At any point on the downswing, including halfway down (your hands just below your waist), you should be able to draw a straight line from the butt end of the club to the ball (FIGURE 7.4). No exceptions. You should imagine that there's a ball in your right hand and you're trying to throw it at the one on the ground.

Figure 5: The hand path should be symmetrical on both sides of the ball, so as your arms reach parallel on the follow-through, your hands should once again be even with your bicep (this time, your left bicep). As you can see here, Zach's hands continue to follow the rotation of the body (FIGURE 7.5) and exit on his shoulder line, just where they were at the top of his backswing.

FIGURE 7.5

Checkpoints for the Shaft Plane

For the shaft to meet the definition of being on-plane, it must be pointing at or parallel to the target line at all points during the swing. No matter where you draw a line from the shaft—through either the hosel or the butt end of the grip—it should point to the target line or be parallel to it. The following eight positions, as demonstrated here by multiple PGA Tour winner Jonathan Byrd, are the ones most easily checked in a mirror or on a video camera.

Figure 1: The shaft is parallel to the ground on the backswing, and the shaft is also parallel to the target line (FIGURE 7.6)

Figure 2: Halfway back (with your left arm parallel to the ground), the butt end of the shaft points to the target line (FIGURE 7.7)

FIGURE 7.6

FIGURE 7.7

Figure 3: At the top of the backswing, the end of the club points to an extension of the target line behind the ball (FIGURE 7.8)

Figure 4: Halfway down (with your hands just below your waist), the shaft lines up with the middle of your right forearm and points to the target line (FIGURE 7.9)

Figure 5: When the shaft is parallel to the ground on the downswing, it's also parallel to the target line (FIGURE 7.10)

FIGURE 7.8

FIGURE 7.9

FIGURE 7.10

FIGURE 7.11

FIGURE 7.12

FIGURE 7.13

Figure 6: At impact, the shaft is pointing to the ball and the target line (FIGURE 7.11)

Figure 7: Halfway through, the shaft is parallel to the ground and the target line (FIGURE 7.12)

Figure 8: At the finish, the shaft is 90 degrees to your spine, bisecting either the eye or the ear line (FIGURE 7.13)

> **PLEASE NOTE...** Ninety percent of all golfers do not have the flexibility to swing the club to parallel at the top of the backswing. If the shaft is short of parallel, it's on-plane as long as the grip end points to the target line (some people think this is laid off). For that matter, even golfers who swing well beyond parallel (for example, John Daly, Phil Mickelson) can still have the shaft on-plane. Daly's swing is so long that the head dips well below the grip at the top, but it still points at the target line and, by definition, is on-plane. Daly's clubhead has to take a longer route back to the ball, but as long as he keeps his hands and the shaft on-plane, it will take a straight line into the ball, generating tremendous clubhead speed.

Checkpoints for the Shoulder Plane

If you were to draw a box around your upper torso and shoulders at the top of the backswing (with your spine in the center of the box), your shoulders should rotate within this inclined box (FIGURES 6.11 and 6.12 from earlier). The thing to remember is that as long as your spine angle remains constant, your shoulders will rotate around it on the same plane. If your head or hips move around during the swing, however, then your spine angle will be compromised and your shoulders will rotate on different angles, causing your hands and arms to compensate.

Checkpoints for the Clubface Plane

As I stated in the previous chapter, the clubface angle is the least important of the four essentials of plane, because it

FIGURE 7.14

merely dictates what your release has to do to square the face. That's why you can have the clubface off-plane (FIGURE 7.14) and still play great golf, provided that you can train your release properly. Ideally, it would be best to have a square or on-plane clubface, but, in extreme cases (too far open or closed), it may need to be changed.

Figure 1: The checkpoint to be most concerned with is at the top of the backswing. At the top, the clubface should match your left forearm (FIGURE 7.8). If it points more to the sky, it's closed; if it points down, it's open. The more extreme the clubface is in either direction, the harder it is to get the release right at the bottom of your swing. If the clubface is extremely open, your hands and forearms have to rotate more to square the clubface; if it's extremely closed, you have to hold off the release more. If it's parallel to your left forearm and your arm is on the same line as your shoulders, then you can just go straight into the ball without having to manipulate the clubface. With the way a club is designed to twist, if the swing is on-plane, the face is easier to rotate properly.

Figure 2: When the shaft is parallel to the ground on the backswing and the downswing, it's ideal to have the toe pointing up to the sky (FIGURE 7.10).

Figure 3: When the shaft is parallel to the ground on the follow-through (post-impact), the clubface should match your spine angle (FIGURE 7.12). The rotation of the clubface after impact should be minimal; most of it should occur prior to impact, when the unhinging and the rotation of the wrists provide an extra burst of speed.

Drills for Hand Path

When performing the following drills on the range, make sure to put down your alignment clubs and mark your ball position with a tee so that you don't lose your spot. Start by making some practice swings at a tee before advancing to more regular speeds with a ball. You want to be able to perform the move consistently with a practice swing before advancing to a full swing. As you progress, consider doubling up two shafts and place them about fifteen feet in front of you, directly on the target line. Begin curving the ball around the makeshift pole, starting the ball to the right of the shafts and drawing them back toward your target line. If you can develop a consistent draw pattern while working on these drills, it'll be that much easier to take your game from the range to the course.

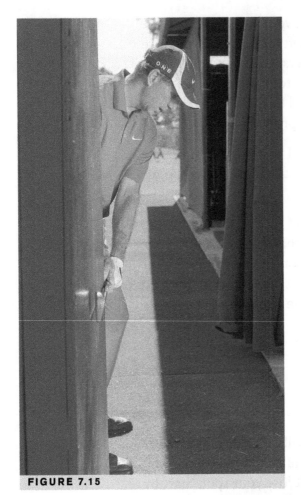

FIGURE 7.15

Shaft to the Wall (for Takeaway)

This is an excellent drill for working on the path of the hands during the takeaway and getting the shaft on-plane as well. Put your left foot up against the left side of a door frame and take your normal address position; your toes should extend beyond the frame. Pivot back until the shaft is flush with the wall and is parallel to the ground, with the club's toe pointing skyward (FIGURE 7.15). You don't want only the clubhead touching the wall (hands out, clubhead in); you want both the shaft and the head lightly touching it, which would be on-plane.

Left Shoulder under Noodle (for Hands at the Top)

The following drill helps you get your hands in position at the top to swing down at the ball in a straight line, which creates the most speed. Put two shafts together and slide a noodle over the top grip. Stick the two shafts in the ground (inclined toward you) and step toward them until the noodle is lightly touching the top of your right shoulder (FIGURE 7.16). (Think of Hogan's pane of glass image, with his head sticking through the glass and the glass resting on his shoulders.) Take a side step about an inch toward the target so that your right shoulder is in front of the noodle, and stick a tee in the ground to mark your ball position. Stick another shaft on your toe line several feet from your right foot, so that when you take your backswing (to parallel), the grip end of the shaft is even with the hosel of your club (FIGURE 7.17).

Now swing to the top: if you rotate properly, your left arm will be on the same angle as your shoulders and your

FIGURE 7.16

FIGURE 7.17

FIGURE 7.18

left arm will stay underneath the noodle (FIGURE 7.18); however, if you lift your arms into an upright position (above your shoulder line), the left arm will bump into the noodle. As long as your left arm is on the same line as your shoulders, then your hands are in the perfect position to attack the ball.

Break the Chicken Wing (for Follow-Through)

About 95 percent of all slicers swing the club across their bodies (to the left) on the downswing, which causes the clubhead to swing from high to low. With that type of swing, the hands and arms do not rotate properly, causing the left elbow to bend like a "chicken wing." If it's your tendency to slice or pull shots, work on the following drill, which will help free up and relax your arms and get rid of that chicken wing.

Put two shafts together with a noodle on one end, and stick the shafts in the ground about a foot outside your left big toe (closer to the target). Make your normal swing but with one slight adjustment: as your hands swing out to the right on the follow-through, have them swing up and over your left shoulder before you turn to the finish (FIGURES 7.19 AND 7.20). Keep your chest facing the ball until your hands are completely over your shoulder, then turn to face the target and finish your swing (FIGURE 7.21). This drill forces the arms to fold without the rotation of your shoulders, which is what causes many golfers to come over the top (and hit the noodle).

FIGURE 7.19

FIGURE 7.20

FIGURE 7.21

Drills for Shaft Plane

Self-Analysis with Impact Bag

Set up to an impact bag (see mikebender.com for how to order one) or a smaller-size tire, and stick a shaft straight into the ground directly in front of it. Address the bag with your feet and shoulders square to your target line and the

FIGURE 7.22

FIGURE 7.23 **FIGURE 7.24**

clubface in the center of the bag, directly in line with the shaft (FIGURE 7.22). Make your normal swing, trying to return the clubface to the middle of the bag; drive the club-head right into the bag as if it were an imaginary ball.

You want the bag to move to the right of the shaft after impact, which means the clubhead is approaching impact from inside the target line—on-plane (FIGURE 7.23). If the bag moves to the left of the shaft, then you're swinging down across your body from out to in (FIGURE 7.24). Should you struggle to move the bag to the right, work on the fol-lowing drills until you can consistently contact the bag from the inside.

Double Shafts
(for Backswing and Downswing)

This is a good drill to help you visualize the correct plane of the shaft—on both the backswing and the downswing. Hold two clubs together, back to back, so that the grip end of the second club is pointing up toward the sky (FIGURE 7.25). Swing both shafts back until they're parallel to the ground: as you do this, the second shaft should slide down your left thigh (FIGURE 7.26). Should you snatch the first shaft to the inside or take it outside, the second shaft will run away from your left leg. Once you feel the shaft on your leg, turn to the top: the butt end of the second club should now point to the target line (FIGURE 7.27). Reverse

FIGURE 7.25

FIGURE 7.26

FIGURE 7.27   **FIGURE 7.28**

direction and swing the butt end of the second club down toward the ball. Just as your hands dip below your waist, the grip end of the club should point directly at the ball (FIGURE 7.28).

Hands to the Wall
(Fix for a "Laid-Off" Shaft)

This exercise prevents you from swinging the club too far to the inside and laying the shaft off at the top, and also promotes a better shaft plane. Set up in your golf posture with your rear end lightly touching a wall. Turn to the top, trying to touch your hands to the wall without banging the clubhead into the wall first (FIGURE 7.29). On the backswing,

FIGURE 7.29

it's better to err on the steep side (with the shaft more upright) versus "laid off" (with the shaft pointing left of the target), because then the club has to shallow out and swing from the inside to get back to the ball. If it's laid off, then it has to get steeper on the downswing, which forces the club to the outside and makes you swing down across the target line.

Empty the Bucket
(Fix for "Crossing the Line")

The following drill is for people who cross the line at the top of their backswing, meaning that the shaft points right of the target line. Take your address position and hold an empty range bucket as if it were half full, with your hands on the side of the bucket. As your shoulders turn back, allow the bucket to move with the pivot of your body (FIGURE 7.30). Continue rotating your shoulders to the top of your backswing motion, gradually dumping the imaginary balls from the bucket over your right shoulder (FIGURE 7.31). On the downswing, drive the end of the bucket toward the ball (FIGURE 7.32).

Golfers who cross the line usually take the club too far inside on the takeaway, dumping the balls out almost immediately; they then lift their arms to the top to complete their backswing, which would cause the balls to dump out on their heads. If the shaft is on the proper plane, and

FIGURE 7.30

FIGURE 7.31

FIGURE 7.32

the left arm is on the same line as the shoulders (at the top), then much like the bucket, you can accelerate your arms and hands in a straight line toward the ball.

Fix for Coming "Over the Bottom" (for Impact)

Some people come "over the top" right away, whereas others come "over the bottom," meaning that the wrists release horizontally, changing the angle of the shaft as it approaches impact. This is also called "tipping out," and results in the shaft jumping off-plane. To fix an over-the-bottom move, stick a shaft and a noodle in the ground and angle it so that the noodle is parallel to the target line. From your address position, move forward until the shaft touches the underside of the noodle. Back up about three fingers (FIGURE 7.33) and take one little step to the left,

FIGURE 7.33

FIGURE 7.34

toward the target (FIGURE 7.34), then place a tee down to mark your ball position.

Make your normal swing, and try to bring the shaft down under the noodle. If you come over the bottom, you'll smack the noodle. Your hands need to continue moving toward the ball, and your wrists need to release vertically so that the shaft approaches the ball on a straight line (FIGURE 7.35). Note: You can add a level of difficulty by putting a shaft and a noodle on your hands to work on the path of the hands, both going back and swinging forward.

FIGURE 7.35

Single Drill for Clubface Plane

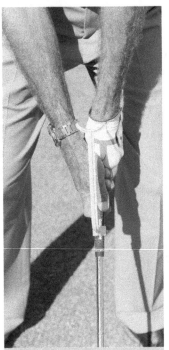

FIGURE 3.36

Square at the Top (with Swingyde)

Few people know what a square clubface looks like at the top of the backswing, or how important it is to the efficiency of your swing. If you can get the face square at the top with your hands in the correct position, then you can swing down into the ball with maximum speed and few compensations. The Swingyde training aid (see mikebender.com on how to order one) will teach you how to reach this ideal top-of-the-backswing position on a regular basis.

Attach the Swingyde to the grip of a mid-iron so that the bottom is about 1 inch from the last knuckle on your right hand (FIGURE 7.36). Make sure that the guidelines on top of the swing aid match the face of the club. Swing the club to the top. If the clubface is square, it will be parallel to your left forearm, and the hook will fit flush on your left forearm (FIGURES 7.37 AND 7.38). (Note: If you have a strong grip, you'll have to cup your left wrist a bit to get the Swingyde to fit your arm.)

FIGURE 3.37

FIGURE 3.38

Drills for Hand and Shaft Planes

Plane Board (for Entire Swing)

The plane board is the best tool around for practicing the plane of the hands and the shaft. Adjust the board to the same angle of the shaft when you're in the address position (FIGURE 7.39). The butt end of the grip should point to your belt line. Swing the shaft back flush along the board until your right elbow starts to fold, at which point the shaft should lose contact with the board (FIGURES 7.40, 7.41, AND 7.42). Continue to rotate your shoulders to the top, swinging your left arm on the same angle as your shoulders (FIGURE 7.43).

FIGURE 7.39

FIGURE 7.40

FIGURE 7.41

FIGURE 7.42

FIGURE 7.43

FIGURE 7.44

FIGURE 7.45

Coming down, your hands should make a straight line toward the ball, and the clubhead, not the shaft, should touch the board (FIGURE 7.44). This is because the hands swing down on a steeper plane than they did going back. At impact, the shaft once again points to the target line (FIGURE 7.45). The follow-through side is symmetrical with that of the backswing. (For instructions on how to build a plane board yourself or for information on purchasing this training aid, please visit my website at mikebender.com.)

Portable Plane Board (for Entire Swing)

This is an excellent drill to start your practice sessions with, and it helps those who have trouble swinging down from the inside become more on-plane. Put two shafts together and stick one end into the ground so that the shafts sit at a 45-degree angle to your target line, at the same angle as your club shaft at address. If you're not sure what 45 degrees is, trace a line in the ground from your imaginary ball position to the target line, which should form a right angle; half of this is 45 degrees.

Set your club right on top of the bottom shaft and slide it up the portable plane board (FIGURE 7.46). Again, your club should maintain contact with the two shafts until your hands are about waist height, at which point the right elbow folds and the shaft begins to move up and in. Swing to the top (FIGURE 7.47) and then down to the imaginary ball, with your hands above the portable shaft and the clubhead below it. When you reach impact, hook the clubhead right under the bottom shaft (FIGURE 7.48). Repeat this two or three times, then get out in front of your practice station and hit a ball.

FIGURE 7.46

FIGURE 7.47

FIGURE 7.48

FIGURE 7.49

Left Arm to 45 Degrees (for Backswing)

This simple drill will provide you with an image of what halfway back should look like when both the shaft and the hands are on-plane. Lay a shaft on the ground at a 45-degree angle to your target line, positioning the handle just outside the little toe of your right foot. Swing halfway back until your left arm is parallel to the ground: your arm should match the 45-degree angle of the shaft on the ground (FIG-URE 7.49), and the butt end of the club should point to an extension of your target line.

Miss the Cone (for the Takeaway and Downswing)

In addition to improving the path of your hands on the takeaway and the angle they take into the ball (from the inside), this drill also stops people from releasing the shaft out at the bottom of the swing, also known as coming "over the bottom." The presence of the cone forces you to unhinge your wrists vertically, so that the shaft can work straight down into the ball. The noodle forces your hands to come into the ball on an exaggerated inside path, which is temporarily okay if you have the opposite problem of coming in too steep.

Slide a swim noodle onto the end of a shaft, then stick the shaft into the ground at a 45-degree angle, so that the noodle faces you. Take your address posture and slowly walk forward until the noodle is nearly touching the tops of your wrists (FIGURE 7.50). Next, take a small step to your left and stick a tee in the ground to mark your ball position. Finally, place a 3-foot-high road cone down so that the base is approximately 2 feet outside your right foot, and the outside edge is even with your toes. (If you were to swing the club halfway back until the shaft was parallel to the ground, the nose of the cone would be about even with the hosel; you can also substitute a shaft for the cone, but the latter is more forgiving.)

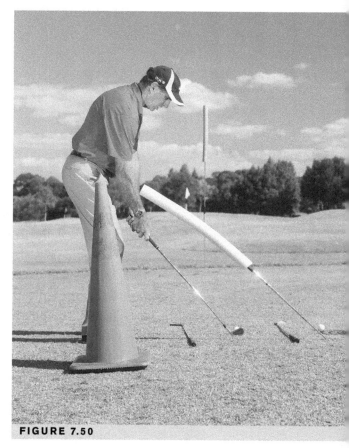

FIGURE 7.50

FIGURE 7.51

FIGURE 7.52

Now you're ready. As you take the club back, your hands should blend in with your left thigh (hands in, clubhead out) and pass about 2 to 3 inches under the noodle (FIGURE 7.51). If you take the club back to the outside, your hands will bump into the noodle; if you suck the clubhead too far inside, the head will bang the cone. Continue to swing to the top—the clubhead should pass outside the cone. As you swing down, the head should swing inside the cone and your hands should pass under the noodle (FIGURE 7.52). If you come over the top with your shoulders on the downswing, then your hands will hit the noodle, and if the club shaft gets too steep, the clubhead will hit the cone.

The Ultimate Practice Station

This exercise will prevent you from releasing the club too soon and will also encourage the proper hand path on the downswing. Remove the two shafts and the noodle on your hands from the preceding drill and stick them in the ground on an angle so that the noodle is lightly touching your right shoulder. Take a small step to the left, toward the target (about 3 inches), and repeat as above. The noodle on your shoulder will prevent you from lifting your arms on the backswing (FIGURE 7.53) and will put your hands in position to swing on a straight line into the golf ball (FIGURE 7.54). You can take this a step further and create the ultimate station, by doubling up two shafts and a noodle and sticking them on your hands, just as before. This forces your hands to move on the proper plane on the takeaway, backswing, and downswing.

FIGURE 7.53

FIGURE 7.54

8

Proper Sequencing of the Arms and Body

The golf swing is a series of circles: the hips make the smallest, tightest circle, followed by the shoulders, the arms, and the clubhead, which makes the largest circle. A simpler way to imagine this would be to picture yourself standing in the

FIGURE 8.1

center of an old 12-inch record LP, with your hips, shoulders, arms, hands, and clubhead working away from the center (FIGURE 8.1). The farther you move out from the center of the record, the bigger the circle each individual piece makes, and the faster it moves. For example: if your hips were moving 5 to 7 miles per hour, then your shoulders would be traveling 10 to 15 mph, your arms 20 to 25 mph, and the clubhead approximately 90 miles per hour (FIGURE 8.2).

With all of these pieces traveling different distances and speeds and at different times, there has to be a perfect sequence in place for everything

FIGURE 8.2

to arrive at the ball in a good impact position—shoulders square, hips open, hands forward, and so on. That is what this chapter is about. There's an arm swing and a body turn, and the two must be blended together, even though at various times during the swing, one is moving while the other is fairly quiet, and vice versa.

The sequencing of the arms and the body is the final element because it's the glue that holds everything together. If you're missing this piece, then the other elements in place are not as effective. You can have good alignment, a perfect setup, and an on-plane backswing, but if your downswing sequencing is incorrect, you're going to struggle to hit the ball with any type of consistency. Gain an understanding of what the correct downswing sequencing looks like, and work on the drills in the next chapter, and you'll have all of the pieces you need to make the most efficient golf swing possible—one whose motion is easy to repeat and has the fewest moving parts.

Three Sources of Movement

There are three independent sources of power capable of moving the golf club—the hips, the shoulders, and the arms/hands. You can rotate your hips back and forth independently, keeping your shoulders and arms still; you can rotate your shoulders back and forth independently from your hips or your arms; and you can swing your arms back and forth independently without moving your hips or shoulders. You will use all three sources during the swing, but how much you use them and when are the keys to getting your sequencing right and making an efficient, on-plane swing. Here's a brief look at all three and what roles they play in the proper sequencing of the body and the arms.

Shoulders

The shoulders start the backswing by rotating, which in turn moves the hands and the arms to the top of the backswing, at which time their job is finished. From here, the hands accelerate at the ball and the shoulders are passive, responding to the acceleration of the arms. They are followers on the downswing, not leaders. Of course, getting the average golfer to keep his or her shoulders passive is quite a challenge, because they're typically the first thing to move on the downswing. When you're trying to hit something with force, it's very natural to want to use your shoulders. They feel very powerful, but, as you'll learn in this chapter, speed is more important in golf than power.

Arms

Their role is the exact opposite of the shoulders', in that they remain very passive on the backswing before turning the afterburners on during the downswing. The arms follow the pivot of the upper body to the top of the backswing, at which point they accelerate the hands in a straight line to the ball. This acceleration of the arms is the key to a fast, efficient downswing. As the arms and the hands fire straight toward the ball, the hips initially respond to the momentum of the arms before taking on a life of their own.

Note: This fast acceleration of the arms can be accomplished only if the tension level in the shoulders and the arms is light. Most amateurs have so much tension that the arms become part of the body and cannot move independently of the shoulders, which causes them to have very little speed.

Hips

The hips, on average, rotate about 45 degrees on the backswing, which helps facilitate a full 90-degree shoulder turn.

FIGURE 8.3

FIGURE 8.4

On the downswing, they begin to unwind automatically in response to the acceleration of the arms until the hands get to about waist height, at which point they really start to accelerate (FIGURE 8.3). The hips, at this point, should make the tightest circle they can, which allows the clubhead to gain more speed (FIGURE 8.4).

Why do the hips turn on the juice at waist height? It's another principle of physics, much like a boat and a water skier. When a boat pulls a water skier, it must first accelerate in a straight line to get the skier out of the water. Once the boat and the skier reach full speed, the boat then makes the sharpest corner it can, which causes the skier to increase his or her speed as they are flung around the boat. In the golf swing, the arms and the hands must initially accelerate as fast as possible in a straight line toward the ball, much as the skier does. As the arms and the hands are reaching full speed, the body (the boat) makes the sharpest circle possible, which allows for maximum acceleration at impact.

The hips also play an important role in helping control the clubface through impact. As long as they're rotating, the handle of the club keeps moving and the clubhead doesn't catch up until several frames after impact, ensuring a solid, downward strike and preventing any flipping or twisting of the clubface.

Easy as 1-2-3, or S-A-H

So there you go: the shoulders start the club back, the arms bring it down, and the hips complete its journey. That's the proper order of sequencing to the golf swing: shoulders, arms, hips. Get that right and apply the three elements you learned earlier, and you'll hit the ball with great speed, accuracy, and consistency.

Backswing Sequence: Shoulders Lead the Way

Most people associate the word *sequence* with the downswing, but there is an order to the way you should bring the club back. Again, the purpose of the backswing is to put your hands and arms in position to swing down to the ball on a direct line, from the inside. This straight-line acceleration is the key to hitting the ball solid—and far.

The shoulders take the lead on the backswing, while the arms and the hips essentially go along for the ride. On the takeaway, the left shoulder rotates down and then across your stance, a full ninety degrees from its starting position. As the shoulders turn, they pull the hips back. The arms simply respond to the pivot of the shoulders; they do not move on their own.

Most golfers take the club back with their hands and arms, because they're the only link we have to the club. There's another reason, too: most everything we do is with our hands and arms, whether it's text messaging someone, drinking a cup of coffee, or throwing an object; thus, as soon as someone picks up a golf club, the natural thing to do is use the hands and the arms. This is why so many people snatch the clubhead back to the inside and have very quick backswings. If you spot someone with a fast backswing, you know the hands and the arms are in control because they're the primary speed generators in the swing. (More on this shortly.)

The other disadvantage to using the hands and the arms on the backswing is that this makes it extremely difficult to keep the hands and the shaft on-plane. Your arms are attached to your shoulders, which have a ball-and-socket joint capable of moving your arms in almost any direction; your wrists are also capable of a wide range of motion. When your hands, wrists, and arms are in charge of the backswing, they can take the club almost anywhere, but if you allow them to be moved by the pivot of your shoulders, they will be more likely to travel on the same plane every time.

As soon as you're done turning the shoulders, your arms should stop as well. Everything (your hands, arms, and shoulders) should arrive at the top together. If your arms keep going after the shoulders stop, then you lose your radius, and it's much harder to sync your arms and body up through impact. The sequencing for the backswing is fairly simple: you get in the correct tilts at address and turn your shoulders around your spine, maintaining the tilts. If you allow your arms and hands to follow and stop when your shoulders do, then everything will be in a perfect position to start the downswing.

What Starts the Downswing?

One of the great debates in golf centers around the question: what starts the downswing? Most golfers would tell you it's the lower body, because they've either read or been instructed that the downswing starts from the ground up. This concept is only partly true. The body's responsibility is to provide resistance for the swing, just as a starting block creates resistance for a sprinter at the start of a race. The runner can explode off the block faster because it's anchored to the track, just as your lower body is fixed to the ground in the golf swing. When your lower body is solid to the ground, it creates resistance to accelerate your hands and arms against.

Despite what they've been told about the lower body, 90 percent of all golfers still use their shoulders to start the downswing. There are several reasons why, the foremost being tension: the more tension you have in your hands and forearms, the more your arms become linked to your body. They can't swing freely, thereby forcing the shoulders to move the club. The shoulders also feel more powerful, and in anything we do where we have to hit something on the ground, it only feels natural to use them. Yet when the shoulders move (or rotate) first on the downswing, they force the hands and the arms out, pulling the club over the top.

So what initiates the downswing? Consider that, in a good backswing (short of parallel), the shoulders turn 90 degrees and the hips about 45; the hands swing in a half circle to the top, about 160 degrees. From here to impact, the shoulders turn back 90 degrees (to return to square), the hips about 70 (because they're open in a good impact position), and the hands another 165 (because the hands are slightly forward at impact). That means the hands have the farthest distance to travel in the quarter of a second it takes to hit the ball on the downswing. So what moves first? It has to be the arms and the hands, because the hands have to travel a much greater distance than the hips and the shoulders do in the same period of time.

The first move down should be an acceleration of the arms and the hands straight toward the ball. Physics tells us that the fastest distance between two objects is a straight line, so for the clubhead to travel the distance it has to in a quarter of a second, the hands need to take a direct route to the ball with minimum compensating moves.

The Match Game

If you were to stand on two feet and jump as high as you could, you would squat down and swing your arms behind you and then forward. Just as your arms passed in front of your body, you would then use the momentum of your arms and spring up with your legs. The golf swing is the same motion: the arms accelerate and as soon as they're down in front of your body (your hands at waist height), the hips accelerate, pulling the shoulders, the arms, and the club around, much as the boat propels the water skier.

This is an example of what we refer to as "matching up." From waist height on the downswing to waist height on the follow-through, the hips have to match the speed (proportionally) of the arms and the club (FIGURES 8.5 AND 8.6).

If the clubhead moves faster than your hips, then the face tends to rotate too much, which can lead to a hook. If the hips spin out way before the hands and the clubhead arrive at impact, then you tend to block the ball out to the right. If the body moves in proportion to the arm swing, however, then you won't get any undue twisting or flipping of the clubhead, and you'll hit the ball fairly straight.

FIGURE 8.5

FIGURE 8.6

Transition: Easy Does It

No part of the swing gives golfers more fits than the transition, or the initial change of direction from backswing to downswing. If your backswing is too fast, it's likely your transition will be too quick as well, which is sure to throw off your sequencing and wreak all sorts of havoc on the downswing.

The arms and the hands initiate the downswing, but they should start down at the same speed they finished the backswing on, which is to say slowly. Think of a roller coaster as it reaches the top of the hill: when it gets there, it creeps over; it doesn't accelerate real fast until a little farther down the track when it's had time to build some speed. The transition works the same way: your shoulder turn takes your arms to the top, then the arms gradually pick up speed as they swing down toward the ball.

Another great analogy for the transition is one of a car in reverse. You drive fairly slow in reverse, but then you have to stop before you throw it into forward gear—otherwise, everyone gets a case of whiplash. Similarly, if your change of direction from the top is too fast, there's a buggy whip to the club that makes it difficult to return the clubface back to square.

What Creates Speed

The way to drive the ball past the rest of your Saturday foursome is to swing your arms and hands as fast as you can. That requires speed, not power, which means using the smaller, fast-twitch muscles in your wrists and forearms to generate speed, not the larger, slower muscles in your upper torso. The analogy I like to use is one of a motorcycle and a four-wheel drive jeep sitting side by side at a red light. Once the light turns green, which one do you think will cover a quarter of a mile in the fastest amount of time? The answer is the much smaller and quicker motorcycle, because although the jeep has a lot more horsepower, it takes a while to get up to speed and has a lot more mass to move around.

Most amateurs associate speed with strength, which is why they grip the club harder and have so much tension in their hands, arms, and shoulders as they swing. They think that if they swing hard enough, the ball will go farther. Yet all that this tension does is slow the clubhead down. A tight muscle is a slow muscle, and a relaxed muscle a fast one, which is why when people swing easy, they always seem to hit the ball farther than expected. There's not as much tension, and they're using their wrists to accelerate the club, versus trying to control it with the bigger, slower muscles.

The wrists produce more speed than any other part of the body, and if you eliminate them from your swing, you have to work really hard to get the clubhead up to speed. Ben Hogan used to say that he'd like to have "three right hands" on the downswing, because of the speed the right arm and the wrist generated as the wrist released and whipped the clubhead through the ball. Most golfers think being "wristy" is bad. This is true in the short game, but in the long game you need to create as much speed as you can, and that means using your wrists as much as you can.

Cracking the Whip for Speed

You can create even more clubhead speed if you learn to apply the concept of "cracking the whip" at the bottom of your swing. There is a braking-and-acceleration motion that occurs on the downswing that allows you to max out your clubhead speed where you need it most, just prior to impact.

The braking occurs when your hands are almost even with the ball, opposite your left thigh. To that point, you want to accelerate your hands as fast as you can toward the ball: this creates an angle between the shaft and your left forearm. When the hands start to slow down, the wrists unhinge and swivel, releasing the angle and the clubhead into the ball and providing an extra burst of speed through impact. You have to stop one joint to transfer energy to another, and the braking of the hands allows the wrists to unhinge and the clubhead to sling-shot its way through the ball, transferring additional energy down into the shaft and the clubhead—just as cracking the whip or snapping a towel does (FIGURES 8.7 AND 8.8).

One analogy I use is that of trying to flick tape off your fingertips. The only way to do it is by snapping your wrists as fast as you can. This is similar to the swiveling action of the

FIGURE 8.7

FIGURE 8.8

wrists at impact, except that in golf you add an element of rotation (of the forearms), which increases your clubhead speed even more.

LPGA Hall of Famer Mickey Wright actually practiced this cracking-of-the-whip technique, according to fellow Hall of Famer Kathy Whitworth. Whitworth once told a story about how Wright would make full swings on the range, trying to hit the ball as far as she could with no follow-through. The rotation and momentum of the body would help carry the club around, but Wright would drive the leading edge of the club right down into the ground, trapping the ball between the face and the turf. As a result, the ball would come off the face like a rocket.

Whoever taught her this drill knew something about physics and the idea of cracking the whip, because the stopping action was created by the braking of the hands just below her waist on the downswing. She was able to apply maximum clubhead speed and force into the back of the ball and then the ground, which explains why she had such tremendous velocity and control over the ball on her shots.

9

How to Practice the Correct Sequencing

The downswing, with all of its individual moving parts (hips, arms, shoulders, and hands), takes about a quarter of a second to complete. That's not even enough time to catch and shoot the ball in an NBA basketball game and still have it count. It's also why the downswing is the trickiest section of the golf swing to train, and why I think it's better practiced in segments.

It's like learning how to play the piano: You start with the individual notes, then you discover how to string the notes together to play a song; you don't just memorize the different keys and go. The same is true of the downswing. You have an arm swing and a body turn, and they have to be blended together so that you can arrive at a good impact position every time.

Sometimes blending the two is anything but easy, however, because there are certain times on the downswing when the arms are accelerating and the body isn't doing much, and vice versa. For example: At the start of the downswing, the arms and the hands gather speed and accelerate toward the ball, while the hips remain fairly passive (they only respond to the acceleration of the arms). But as the hands reach about waist height, the hips start to fire and the hands begin to brake, transferring additional speed down through the shaft to the clubhead. A few examples of this would be cracking a whip or snapping a towel.

Scan this code to view a video demonstrating proper swing sequencing at the author's website: mikebender.com.

The arms and the body travel in different-size circles and at different speeds on the downswing, so there is no way to make them work together for the entire quarter of a second it takes to hit the ball. Yet at the moment of truth (at impact), they have to be moving in proportion with one another in order to deliver the clubface square to the ball with maximum velocity. That's another reason why the sequencing should be trained in two parts, because if there's symmetry between the halfway-down and the halfway-through positions, then, chances are, everything is arriving at the ball as it should.

The following drills will train you, first, how to accelerate your arms and hands toward the ball (without rotating the upper body too soon, which is the most common mistake), and second, how to fire your hips correctly at the right moment. Some exercises will work both. Once you have all of the notes running in order, you can make beautiful music with your downswing.

Part 1: Arms and Hands Accelerate toward the Ball

Right Hand Ball Toss Drill

The purpose of this drill is for you to train your arms and hands to move first without turning your shoulders out, which is what most amateurs do at the start of the downswing.

Set up with a ball in your right hand (no club), and put the palm of your left hand flat against your right shoulder and push. Pivot to the top (FIGURE 9.1), and fire the ball in your right hand at the one on the ground, accelerating your right arm down toward the ball as you hold your right shoulder back (FIGURE 9.2). You should be able to hit the ball on the ground at least three out of five times. Imagine that you're holding a club and try to feel as if you're putting the clubhead on the back of the ball.

FIGURE 9.1

FIGURE 9.2

Sidearm Toss Drill

This is an extension of the previous drill, and it trains you to accelerate your right arm toward the ball and rotate your hips without opening your shoulders up, which is the most common sequencing fault of amateurs. Get in your normal golf posture, with a ball in your right hand and your left hand resting on top of a club. Swing your right arm to the top (FIGURE 9.3), then throw the ball sidearm, level with the ground. Release the ball so that it goes straight out, parallel to the ground, as you extend your right arm straight toward the target (FIGURE 9.4). Try to rotate your hips as much as you can without losing your connection to the ground and your posture.

FIGURE 9.3

FIGURE 9.4

FIGURE 9.5   **FIGURE 9.6**

Right Toe Up Drill

The following drill trains you to accelerate your arms toward the ball while keeping your hips fairly passive at the start of the downswing. Take your normal address position, and lift the toes of your right foot off the ground so that only your heel is touching. Swing to the top and down, but don't rotate onto the inside of your right foot and set the toes down until the clubhead contacts the ball (FIGURES 9.5 AND 9.6). This prevents you from firing your hips early at the start of the downswing, so your arms and hands move down first. The hips respond to the acceleration of the arms; they don't lead the arms.

Square Hips, Shoulders Drill

This drill forces you to use your arms on the downswing and also gives you a feel for hitting against a firm left side, which provides resistance so that you can accelerate your hands and arms and maximize your clubhead speed. You can't have a firm left side if you open up your shoulders too soon. Make your normal backswing, but as you change direction and swing forward, keep both feet planted on the ground and your hips and shoulders square (parallel) to the target line (FIGURE 9.7). Because you're not using your hips, your shoulders won't open up after impact, and the club will swing up over your left shoulder into the finish (FIGURE 9.8).

FIGURE 9.7 **FIGURE 9.8**

FIGURE 9.9   **FIGURE 9.10**

Basketball Drop Drill

The following drill also encourages the proper downswing sequencing of the arms and the body. Place a basketball between your legs, just above your knees, and assume your normal address position. Pivot to the top, and as soon as you start down, drop the ball down from your legs and swing through. For the ball to drop, you must be holding your right leg and hip back, which helps get your arms moving down and in front of your body. That's the first move, and the correct move: the right side holds, while the left hip begins to clear (that is, open), which causes the legs to gap and the ball to drop (FIGURES 9.9 AND 9.10).

Most golfers initiate the downswing by turning their hips or, in many cases, rotating their right shoulder out toward the target line, which brings the legs closer together and prevents the ball from dropping. You want to keep your legs stable and use the resistance of the ground to accelerate your arms and hands. If you do this, your transition will be perfect, and the ball should immediately drop.

Club Upside-Down Drill

This drill is for people with overactive shoulders on the downswing. Hold a club upside-down in your right hand so that you're gripping it by the hosel, and extend your left arm out away from you so that it's perpendicular to your target line. Swing the handle back to the top (FIGURE 9.11), then fire it down toward the ground (the imaginary ball position) with your right arm and hand. Try to keep your left arm still during the entire swing, which prevents your shoulders from twisting open.

The handle should make a loud "swoooosh" sound as it's swinging closest to the ground. Also, as the shaft comes to a stop, it should bisect a point between your neck and left shoulder (FIGURE 9.12). Most golfers use their shoulders too much, which causes the shaft to swing down and across (toward the body) and finish somewhere between their belt line and left arm. Accelerate your arms from

FIGURE 9.11

FIGURE 9.12

the start and keep your shoulders passive, and the shaft will finish closer to your neck.

Accelerate and Brake Drill

This drill helps you achieve maximum speed where you need it most—at impact. Hold a club upside down by the hosel with both hands, and swing to the top. Next, swing the shaft down as fast as you can into a good impact position and hold (no follow-through), with your hands remaining ahead of the

FIGURE 9.13

handle (FIGURE 9.13). If you can maintain this relationship and still get the handle to make a "swoooosh" sound near the ground, then you're applying maximum speed and energy at the point of impact.

It's similar to the concept of "cracking the whip." As you swing down, you want your hands to accelerate as fast as they can in a straight line toward the ball. As your hands approach impact, however, they begin to brake, which causes the wrists to unhinge and swivel, transferring energy to the clubhead. The laws of physics say that to accelerate one joint, you must stop another, and just like cracking the whip, the abrupt slowing of the hands sends an additional burst of energy down the shaft to the clubhead.

Thump the Sand Drill

This drill promotes the proper downswing sequencing and release point of the club at impact. It's similar to snapping a towel—the hands have to stop to accelerate the end. Draw three equal-length lines in the sand, each about six to eight feet long; each line represents your ball position (FIGURE 9.14). Set up to the first line and, with your left hand only, make a three-quarter backswing and drive the club's leading edge into the sand, on the front side of the line (FIGURE 9.15). Make sure the handle is in front of the clubhead at impact and "thump" the sand, with no follow-through. Work your way down the line, leaving the clubhead in the sand. Repeat this using your right hand only on the second line (FIGURES 9.16 AND 9.17) and using both hands on the third line.

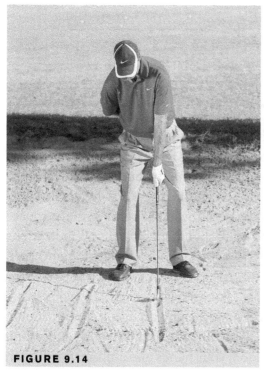

FIGURE 9.14

FIGURE 9.15

FIGURE 9.16

FIGURE 9.17

Part 2: The Hips Fire; Body, Arms Match Up

Two-Piece Downswing

This drill breaks the downswing into two segments, which makes it easier to move your arms and body properly, in good sequence. Swing the club up to the top and then down, stopping when your hands are just below waist height. At this point, the club should be pointing at the ball, your hips square to the target line, and your shoulders closed—all indications of a good transition (FIGURE 9.18). Pause for a moment, then release the clubhead through the ball, firing your hips sharply to the left as if they were taking a tight corner. Stop your swing when your hands are waist height on the follow-through, matching your halfway down position. If your sequencing through impact was good, your hands and club shaft will be in front of your chest, matching up with your hips (FIGURE 9.19).

FIGURE 9.18

FIGURE 9.19

FIGURE 9.20   **FIGURE 9.21**

The Pump Drill

This is an extension of the Two-Piece Downswing Drill. First, take the club up to a normal top-of-backswing position, then move your hands toward the ball, stopping at waist height (the same as the previous drill). Immediately take the club back to the top, then pump it down to the waist-height position once again (FIGURE 9.20). Make sure the hips are responding to the pumping action of the arms, which should take them back to square (that is, address). On the third pump, go ahead and hit the ball (FIGURE 9.21), stopping at waist height on the follow-through. By pumping your arms back and forth and making a swing, you keep your arms relaxed and encourage the proper downswing sequence of arms first, hips second.

Two-Piece Finish Drill

This drill encourages the proper amount of hip rotation through impact. Get yourself in a good impact position, with your hands forward of the clubhead, hips slightly open and shoulders square (FIGURE 9.22). From here, push the ball forward along the ground, using your hips (FIGURES 9.23 AND 24). It's important that the hips continue turning after impact, as this keeps the handle moving and discourages the clubhead from catching up and passing your hands prematurely (that is, flipping the clubhead upward through impact).

If there's no twisting or flipping of the clubhead after impact and your body and arms are matching up, you'll make solid contact. Once the shaft is parallel to the ground, go ahead and finish your swing by rehinging your wrists and allowing your elbows to fold. Your hips should pull your arms and shoulders around, with the arms folding and eventually exiting along the line of your shoulders.

FIGURE 9.22

FIGURE 9.23

FIGURE 9.24

FIGURE 9.25　　　　　　**FIGURE 9.26**

Impact Pose Drill

This isometric exercise teaches you how to get your arms, body, and club in a good impact position. Take your setup and swing the club back to the top. Bring the club down slowly into a good impact position and hold. Check to see that your hips are slightly open and your shoulders square; your right forearm should be lower than your left and your hands forward of the ball (FIGURE 9.25). Get a feel for where your body is at this moment, especially your hips, arms, and shoulders, then start your swing (from impact) and let it rip. The feel should stick with you long enough for you to return the clubhead back to the ball in a good impact position (FIGURE 9.26), which can't happen without proper sequencing.

There's a second version of this exercise, in which you set up and go directly to the posed impact position. You hold this for a few seconds, return to your address position, and then swing without hesitation. You need to start the swing right away while your body still feels the correct impact position.

Waist Height to Waist Height Drill

This drill helps sync up the arms with the body through the most important area—the impact zone. Swing the arms back to waist height on the backswing (FIGURE 9.27), then through to waist height on the follow-through (FIGURES 9.28 AND 9.29). When the hands and the club come through, they should finish directly in front of your body; if the shoulders are turning too much, the hands will finish way left of your body. Your head should also be behind the ball, as it was at address. The goal in the second part of the downswing is to match the arms to the body turn. This is much easier to achieve than the first

FIGURE 9.27   **FIGURE 9.28**

FIGURE 9.29

part, which is getting the arms to work down at the ball before the upper body turns.

Touch and Go Drill

This drill trains the sequencing of the arms and the body, from the takeaway through impact. Set up to a wall with the outside of your left foot touching the wall. Grip a club upside-down

FIGURE 9.30

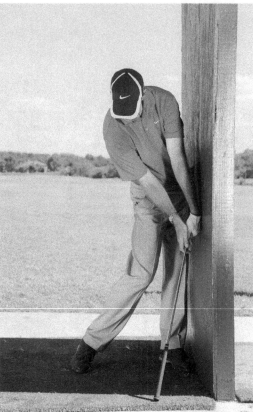

FIGURE 9.31

and then swing it to the top (FIGURE 9.30). As soon as the butt end of the club touches the wall, swing down into an imaginary impact position with the back of your left hand and your left hip touching the wall, and your upper body leaning away from the wall (FIGURE 9.31). Hold this position for several seconds.

The typical amateur has a hard time touching his left hand and hips to the wall at impact. He either spins the left hip away from the ball early on the downswing or rotates his shoulders too soon from the top, which causes the clubhead to release early and pass the hands prematurely. In either of these cases, it causes the clubhead to meet the wall before the hands do.

10

How to Practice and Make a Swing Change

I was giving a lesson one day when I informed my student that I was going to put his swing on video, something I do with all first-time students. "Which swing do you want to see?" he asked. Somewhat perplexed, I replied, "Well, how many do you have?" "Five," he said. Given that we had only an hour, I said, "I don't have time for all five, but let's see three of them." He then proceeded to demonstrate all three swings.

As we went into the Academy, I asked him to tell me the differences in his three swings. He said the first was his "Jack Nicklaus swing," which included a high backswing, a big leg drive, and a very high finish; the second was his baseball swing, which was flatter and more around his body, similar to Ben Hogan's; and the third was his compact swing, in which he tried to keep his right elbow tucked in. As we started to review each swing, a look of embarrassment and then frustration came across his face once he realized that all three were the same. He thought for sure they were all unique because his feel for each of them was very different.

He's not alone. When amateurs head to the range to work on their swing, they usually draw their own conclusions based on what they see (such as the ball flight) and feel. They hit ball after ball after ball until they get a visual or internal confirmation that the swing they're making is working. Mostly, they go by feel, but just because you feel it happening doesn't mean it's real.

I'll give you another example: I was conducting a golf school in Detroit and decided to capture one of the student's swings on video. When I showed it to her, she was defiant. "That's not me," she said. I replied, "It certainly looks like you, because you're wearing the same clothes." She fired back, "I don't swing like that." I said, "Well, how do you swing?" Her response was: "I don't know, but it isn't like that."

These two stories are prime examples of this flaw in perception: what you feel versus what's real. As Tom Kite, one of the hardest workers ever to play the game said, "You learn mechanics first, then learn feel from mechanics, not the other way around." If the mechanics aren't right, the feeling can't be correct.

How do you know your mechanics are right? First, you need feedback so that you know whether you're performing the move correctly. That's what the many practice stations and drills in the "How To" chapters in this book are designed to

Scan this code to view a video demonstrating how to practice at the author's website: mikebender.com.

do (FIGURE 10.1). Second, you need to give your swing the eye test. When you see it on video, it should start to look a whole lot better. For example, the clubhead should be approaching the ball more from the inside, instead of out and over the top, and the motion should look more fluid and efficient.

FIGURE 10.1

Of course, not everybody has access to a video camera, nor do people know what they're looking for when they analyze their swing. Most amateurs would fall in this category, which is why learning how to practice is just as valuable as learning what to practice. You need to know how to set up practice stations and use feedback, so that you're putting in quality time on your swing and moving in a direction that will allow you to achieve your goals faster. Whether you have sixty minutes per week to practice or six hours, the following tips and guidelines will show you how to best use that time and put yourself on the road to improvement.

Exaggeration and Feedback

One of the most frequent questions I get from students is, "How long is this swing change going to take me?" I ask them, "What's your alternative?" Most golfers fall under the definition of insanity, which, to me, means doing the things they always do and expecting different results. Real change requires doing something different, and that begins with instruction and correct practice.

From my own experience and having taught thousands of golfers of all different skill levels, I know that the two fastest ways to make a swing change are exaggeration and feedback. All golfers have the swing they do because they've performed it over and over again, forming what is commonly known as muscle memory. They've repeated the swing so many times that it feels natural to them, so, unless they take some extreme measures, they're going to revert back to the old comfortable swing, even if they feel something different. To override this history, you have to derail the electrical impulses that make you swing this way and send them down another track. You have to create a new memory, or impulse, that is stronger than the original.

The most effective way to rewire your swing is by exaggerating the move you're trying to make on the proper side of how to do it. When I was trying to earn my PGA Tour card in the early 1980s, my swing wasn't as consistent as it needed to be, so I paid a visit to world-renowned instructor David Leadbetter here in Orlando. After watching my swing on film, Leadbetter said I needed to bring my arms down on the backswing. He said they were "too high," causing me to slide my hips and drop the club to the inside on the downswing. After our lesson, I went back home and spent the entire week trying to feel my arms lower on the backswing.

I returned to his academy a week later, and there wasn't much visual change on video, even though I felt as if there was. This went on for three months, and I got so mad I nearly quit the game. Finally, I said, "Enough is enough," and started to exaggerate the movement by swinging my hands around my waist, à la Doug Sanders. I immediately began to shank the ball and take some big, fat divots, but I didn't care as long as the next time I appeared on video, my arm swing was flatter. As I drove over to Leadbetter's academy, I was thinking, "I've really overcooked this," but when he took a look at my swing, the first words out of his mouth were, "Oh, perfect. You finally made the swing change!"

I couldn't believe how much I had to exaggerate the flatter arm swing just to reach the middle ground and make the swing change Leadbetter was proposing. I needed more than three months and a lot of frustration to learn what it really took from a "feel" standpoint to make a swing change.

There are always sides that are better to err on. For example, it's better to aim too far left than right or to swing down too much from the inside than from the outside. If your fault is coming over the top with your shoulders, then you have to exaggerate the opposite movement, which is keeping them closed to the target for as long as possible on the downswing. The practice station with the road cone in chapter 7 will force this exaggeration, because the closer you move the cone to your right foot, the longer the shoulders have to stay closed for the club to swing down underneath the cone. The more you can combine exaggeration with feedback, the sooner the exaggerated move will become the predominant path (that is, memory) and will help you master your swing change.

Positive and Negative Feedback

FIGURE 10.2

If you slide a noodle on the end of a shaft and position the noodle just above your hands (at address), you have to swing your hands down on an extreme inside path; otherwise, they'll bump the noodle. The noodle is an example of negative feedback: if you whack it on the downswing, then you know you're performing the move incorrectly.

There are two types of feedback—negative and positive. Of the two, the negative is the most influential and the one most commonly used in the practice stations throughout this book. You can tell children to say "please" or "thank you," but chances are you'll have to remind them a hundred times before it becomes second nature to them. If they touch their hands on a hot stove, however, you won't have to tell them not to do it again. That's negative feedback: you bump into something (such as running the shaft into the wall) you don't want to hit, and it registers quickly (FIGURE 10.2).

Positive feedback is showing your son or daughter how to sit up properly at the dinner table, or demonstrating to a student over and over again how the left arm, shaft, and club-face should form a straight line at the top of the backswing. You can strap something onto your body, such as the Swingyde (SEE CHAPTER 7), to help you achieve the proper clubface position at the top, and that would be positive feedback. Anything you want to touch to your body is positive feedback (FIGURE 10.3). If I wanted you to shorten your backswing and, in the process of the drill, you ran the clubhead into the wall, that would be negative feedback; however, if I told you to touch the wall with the grip end of the club and then swing down, that would be a source of positive feedback.

FIGURE 10.3

As I said earlier, feedback combined with exaggeration will help you make a swing change in the shortest amount of time. If you rely on feel or practice only the perfect positions, you'll have a hard time making the change. The biggest mistake amateurs make is thinking that a good swing is supposed to feel good in the beginning or when you first make the change. For a player who has a poor swing to begin with and then makes a good swing, it should feel very different. You have to remember that nothing is natural in golf until you repeat it over and over and over.

The Value of Using Training Aids

When I played on the PGA Tour, I was one of only a handful of guys who used training aids. I used a strap around my body to keep my arms in, and I received a lot of strange looks. Yet now, no one says anything when Zach Johnson sets up his portable plane board (two shafts together, SEE CHAPTER 7) on the range or works with a Swingyde attached to his forearm. Everyone sticks shafts into the ground and uses one training aid or another, because golfers understand the value of feedback and what it takes to improve (FIGURE 10.4).

If you're working on your swing and you have the ability to set up these practice stations on the range—shafts, noodles, cones, and all—don't be shy. Do it. You may attract some attention, but chances are, the guy hitting balls next to you will have his own practice station the next time you see him.

You should always lay shafts on the ground for alignment purposes, but, if you can, I strongly recommend combining two shafts and sticking them in the ground about 15 feet forward of where you're hitting, directly on your ball-target line. Zach never works on his swing at home without sticking

FIGURE 10.4

FIGURE 10.5

this makeshift pole out there. The entire time he's out there hitting balls, he's trying to produce a draw without crossing his line (the ball-target line). Everything to the right of the pole is green, and everything to the left is red. Zach's goal is to start each shot out to the right of the pole, in the green zone, and still have it finish in the green. The ball should curve gently from right to left without ever crossing into the red zone. Zach has hit so many balls in practice this way, it's no wonder that he repeatedly ranks among the most accurate drivers on Tour. What's amazing, however, is that for some-one who draws the ball, Zach's drives rarely wander off into the left rough. He prides himself on being one of the best at not missing left.

Zach hits only two or three fades per tournament; his only goal is not to cross his line, which he rarely does (FIGURE 10.5). He has a lot of confidence standing on the tee because he knows what the ball is going to do before he hits it. He also knows what it's not going to do, which is stray too far left. It's hard to play golf if you aim down the middle of the fairway, not knowing which direction the ball will take.

FIVE STEPS TO LEARNING

When you make a swing change, there's a natural process that you must go through, as with learning any motor skill. These five steps govern how you should practice when using exaggeration and feedback to make a swing change.

1. Learn the concept. What changes do you have to make and why do you have to make them? And the concept should make sense: For example, if you line up parallel left, then you can swing on the correct path from the inside, versus aiming to the right and swinging from outside to inside.

2. Perform the new moves in a practice swing with ease. If you cannot perform a new move with little difficulty in a practice swing, then it will be impossible to perform it with a ball.

3. Perform each move on the driving range (hitting balls) with a high degree of consistency. When you can accomplish this, then you're ready for the next step.

4. Perform the new skill on the course with a high degree of consistency. This step may take the greatest amount of time to accomplish, so don't be afraid to retrace your steps and visit steps two and three again.

5. Perform the skill with consistency under competitive conditions, when the pressure is highest. If you don't play in any tournaments, simulate pressure by making a friendly wager with your playing partner on a particular shot or outcome.

Most people want to learn the concept and jump right to the course, skipping steps two and three. You cannot skip steps. If you want to take your new swing concept from the range to the course and be successful, you have to first develop consistency with it on the range. One thing is for sure: if you cannot consistently perform your new swing on the range, it will never happen on the course.

Quality over Quantity

When you're working in these practice stations, there are a few other things you ought to remember. First, before you put any clubs down and set up your feedback station, aim at three different targets (one left, one middle, one right) and practice your alignment. It takes only a few minutes, and it helps calibrate your eyes so that you know what good alignment looks like. Once you set up your practice station, hit ten balls, then walk out in front of the station and hit two balls. The idea is to recreate the same swing without the feedback tools. Finally, never practice one skill for more than an hour. Making a swing change requires a high degree of focus, which starts to suffer if all you do is hit balls in rapid succession.

It takes only 1½ seconds to hit a shot, so if you hit one hundred balls on the range, multiply that number by 1.5 and divide by 60 (minutes), you're getting only 2½ minutes of practice for every 100 balls you hit. That makes those 2½ minutes very, very important. Of course, not everybody has 2 or 3 hours to practice, let alone 60 minutes. If your time is limited, but you can set aside 60 minutes per week, spend half of that time working on your full swing and the other half on your short game. Once you get your swing change down, you can spend more time on your short game and putting, as the pros do. When you're working on your swing, set aside a few minutes to practice your aim (see the previous section) and the plane of your hands and the club shaft. Set up your portable plane board (two shafts on a 45-degree angle; SEE CHAPTER 7), sliding the club up the two shafts and then bringing it down inside the shafts, hooking it underneath at impact.

Next, set up your practice station and hit balls, curving each one around the makeshift pole set along your target line. Identify a start line (to the right of the pole) and a finish line for each shot. If you're hitting to a flagstick, identify an area—or a zone—that you want the ball to finish in. For example, when I asked five-time PGA Tour winner Jonathan Byrd what he considered to be a good shot for a wedge or a 9-iron, he said, "Anything inside 15 feet of the flag or closer." For an 8- or a 7-iron, it was 20 feet; for a 6- or a 5-iron, 25 feet; and for a 4-iron or a rescue club, 35 feet or closer. The point is, he never tried to knock down the pin, as most amateurs do. He identified a zone he wanted to hit the ball into, and that's how he measured his performance. This also makes it easier for him to take his game from the range to the course, because he's identified a zone for each club, and he knows what a good result is.

The zone is always on the side of the pin that is your stock shot. If you like to draw the ball, then the zone is on the right side of the pin, and if you prefer to fade it, then the zone is on the left side of the pin. I suggest hitting groups of ten balls with the ultimate goal of hitting seven out of ten in your zone. The better you get at hitting to a zone, the more consistent and accurate your shots will be on the course.

Take a look at the drills in the book and determine which one helps the most with the changes you're trying to make. If you hit balls for thirty minutes without any feedback, you're only getting exercise. But if the limited minutes you spend practicing are quality minutes, you'll achieve your goals faster than someone who spends three times the amount of effort practicing without a purpose (that is, without feedback).

Warm-Up versus Practice

Thirty minutes prior to play is not the time to be working on swing mechanics; it's a good time, however, to check your aim, hit a few balls, and see whether you can establish a good rhythm and tempo for the day. That's what a warm-up is designed to help you do—get yourself mentally and physically ready to play eighteen holes.

Zach always stretches prior to his pre-round warm-up. When he gets to the range, he opens his session by hitting some easy 110-yard shots with his pitching wedge. Zach normally hits this wedge 125 yards, so by taking 15 yards off, it helps him to swing slower and establish a good tempo and rhythm for his swing. He'll then hit some shots with his even-numbered irons (8, 6, 4) before advancing to the driver. The whole time, he's working on shaping his shots from right to left (about 5 yards), without crossing his line into the red zone. Zach finishes the range part of his warm-up with some touch-and feel shots (30, 40 yards) before going to the putting green. He never works on his swing mechanics prior to a round. He may revisit them after a round, but the time spent before the round is solely for getting himself as ready to play as possible.

One Final Word

It takes time to make a swing change. After Tiger won the Masters and three other PGA Tour events in 1997, he overhauled his swing under the tutelage of Butch Harmon, and it took a full season for him to become his dominating self again (Woods won only once in 1998). It took Zach two to three years to get all of the changes we made down to the point where he was in full maintenance mode.

How long it takes you to make a swing change depends on what it is you're trying to change and also on the number of repetitions and amount of work you put in. After one season, I told Zach he needed to work on getting the shaft on a better plane at the top of the backswing. Using the Bucket Drill in chapter 7 (dumping the imaginary balls over his right shoulder), he needed about a week to get it down. It doesn't take as long to make a backswing change as it does a downswing one, because it's a much slower motion. Because of this, I've had some students make a backswing change in as few as two weeks.

If you commit to the concepts, the principles, and the drills outlined in this book, you will improve in time, and your potential will be unlimited. By unlimited, I mean there's no limit to how much better you can get. I'll give you an example: I had one guy come to me in his first lesson and declare, "If I could just break 100, I'd be happy." Then, as soon as he started to shoot in the 90s consistently, he said to me, "You know, if I could just break 90, I'd be happy." The point is, if you take a direction that includes solid technical information and you practice it correctly, you're going to get better and continue to improve. And that's a fun way to play golf.

INDEX

NOTE: Page references in *italics* indicate figures.

Mike Bender is one of Golf Digest's 50 Best Teachers in America (ranked 4th) and one of Golf Magazine's Top 100 Teachers. The 2009 PGA National Teacher of the Year, Bender has coached more than two-dozen Tour professionals, including 2007 Masters champion Zach Johnson. Before teaching full-time, he competed for three years on the PGA Tour and was a three-time NCAA All-American and two-time NCAA Division III individual champion.

Dave Allen has spent more than a dozen years as an instruction writer/editor for Golf Magazine, Golf for Women magazine, and GolfChannel.com. He has cowritten several golf books, including Play Golf the Pebble Beach Way and Golf Annika's Way.

From one of *Golf Digest*'s 50 Best Teachers in America— a simple, scientific program to develop a repeatable swing

Most golf instruction is based on helping students emulate the best players, but, as Mike Bender puts it, would you rather fly in an airplane that was built by engineers who understood the principles of lift and acceleration, or would you rather fly in one built by people who simply went out to the airport and watched them taking off and landing?

Bender, the 2009 PGA National Teacher of the Year, believes that physics provides a better model for developing a swing that is as efficient, consistent, and timeless as that of Iron Byron, the mechanical robot developed by the USGA to test clubs and balls. Having coached two dozen Tour professionals, including 2007 Masters champ Zach Johnson, Bender shows you how to put the secrets of science into your own swing with a simple, proven program that will take your play to a different level and transform your approach to the game. Once you develop a scientific swing, it's your own game that will really soar.

This book includes links to videos of the author demonstrating key lessons, such as the proper alignment and the swing plane.

TRADE PAPER
PRESS

Also available
as an e-book

ISBN 978-1-63026-901-2
90000

9 781630 269012